# BODY PIERCING
# AND TATTOOS

# Body Piercing and Tattoos

## EXAMINING POP CULTURE

**J.D. LLOYD,** Book Editor

**Daniel Leone,** President
**Bonnie Szumski,** Publisher
**Scott Barbour,** Managing Editor
**James D. Torr,** Series Editor

GREENHAVEN
PRESS ®

THOMSON
★
GALE ™

San Diego • Detroit • New York • San Francisco • Cleveland
New Haven, Conn. • Waterville, Maine • London • Munich

*For more information, contact*
Greenhaven Press
27500 Drake Rd.
Farmington Hills, MI 48331-3535
Or you can visit our Internet site at http://www.gale.com

Cover photo: Dawn Russell
Corel Corporation, 25
Photodisc, 58

LIBRARY OF CONGRESS CATALOGING-IN-PUBLICATION DATA

Body piercing and tattoos / J.D. Lloyd, book editor.
   p. cm.—(Examining pop culture)
Includes bibliographical references and index.
ISBN 0-7377-1059-4 (pbk. : alk. paper) — ISBN 0-7377-1060-8 (lib. : alk. paper)
   1. Tattooing. 2. Body piercing. 3. Body marking. I. Lloyd, J.D., 1959– .
II. Examining pop culture.
GT2345 .B63   2003
391.6'5—dc21                                        2002019387

# CONTENTS

thoughtful consideration to the procedure, the artist, and the design.

munal identity, serving as marks of initiation, candidacy, and group membership. Wearers also ascribe certain mythic and aesthetic qualities to their designs.

# Chapter 4: The Controversial Nature of Body Art

# FOREWORD

POPULAR CULTURE IS THE COMMON SET OF ARTS, entertainments, customs, beliefs, and values shared by large segments of society. Russel B. Nye, one of the founders of the study of popular culture, wrote that "not until the appearance of mass society in the eighteenth century could popular culture, as one now uses the term, be said to exist." According to Nye, the Industrial Revolution and the rise of democracy in the eighteenth and nineteenth centuries led to increased urbanization and the emergence of a powerful middle class. In nineteenth-century Europe and North America, these trends created audiences for the popular arts that were larger, more concentrated, and more well off than at any point in history. As a result, more people shared a common culture than ever before.

The technological advancements of the twentieth century vastly accelerated the spread of popular culture. With each new advance in mass communication—motion pictures, radio, television, and the Internet—popular culture has become an increasingly pervasive aspect of everyday life.

Popular entertainment—in the form of movies, television, theater, music recordings and concerts, books, magazines, sporting events, video games, restaurants, casinos, theme parks, and other attractions—is one very recognizable aspect of popular culture. In his 1999 book *The Entertainment Economy: How Mega-Media Forces Are Transforming Our Lives*, Michael J. Wolf argues that entertainment is becoming the dominant feature of American society: "In choosing where we buy French fries, how we relate to political candidates, what airline we want to fly, what pajamas we choose for our kids, and which mall we want to buy them in, entertainment is increasingly influencing every one of those choices. . . . Multiply that by the billions of choices that, collectively, all of us make each day and you have a portrait of a society in which entertainment is one of its leading institutions."

It is partly this pervasive quality of popular culture that makes it worthy of study. James Combs, the author of *Polpop: Politics and Popular Culture in America*, explains that examining popular culture is important because it can shape people's attitudes and beliefs:

> Popular culture is so much a part of our lives that we cannot deny its developmental powers. . . . Like formal education or family rearing, popular culture is part of our "learning environment.". . . Though our pop culture education is informal—we usually do not attend to pop culture for its "educational" value—it nevertheless provides us with information and images upon which we develop our opinions and attitudes. We would not be what we are, nor would our society be quite the same, without the impact of popular culture.

Examining popular culture is also important because popular movies, music, fads, and the like often reflect popular opinions and attitudes. Christopher D. Geist and Jack Nachbar explain in *The Popular Culture Reader*, "the popular arts provide a gauge by which we can learn what Americans are thinking, their fears, fantasies, dreams, and dominant mythologies. The popular arts reflect the values of the multitude."

This two-way relationship between popular culture and society is evident in many modern discussions of popular culture. Does the glorification of guns by many rap artists, for example, merely reflect the realities of inner-city life, or does it also contribute to the problem of gun violence? Such questions also arise in discussions of the popular culture of the past. Did the Vietnam protest music of the late 1960s and early 1970s, for instance, simply reflect popular antiwar sentiments, or did it help turn public opinion against the war? Examining such questions is an important part of understanding history.

Greenhaven Press's *Examining Pop Culture* series provides students with the resources to begin exploring these questions. Each volume in the series focuses on a particular aspect of popular culture, with topics as varied as popular culture itself. Books in the series may focus on a particular genre, such as *Rap and Hip Hop*, while others may cover a specific medium, such as *Computers and the Internet*. Volumes such as *Body Piercing and Tattoos* have their focus on recent trends in popular culture, while titles like *Americans' Views About War* have a broader historical scope.

In each volume, an introductory essay provides a general

overview of the topic. The selections that follow offer a survey of critical thought about the subject. The readings in *Americans' Views About War*, for example, are arranged chronologically: Essays explore how popular films, songs, television programs, and even comic books both reflected and shaped public opinion about American wars from World War I through Vietnam. The essays in *Violence in Film and Television*, on the other hand, take a more varied approach: Some provide historical background, while others examine specific genres of violent film, such as horror, and still others discuss the current controversy surrounding the issue.

Each book in the series contains a comprehensive index to help readers quickly locate material of interest. Perhaps most importantly, each volume has an annotated bibliography to aid interested students in conducting further research on the topic. In today's culture, what is "popular" changes rapidly from year to year and even month to month. Those who study popular culture must constantly struggle to keep up. The volumes in Greenhaven's *Examining Pop Culture* series are intended to introduce readers to the major themes and issues associated with each topic, so they can begin examining for themselves what impact popular culture has on their own lives.

CONSPICUOUS ON POP SINGERS, BASKETBALL players, movie stars, and even children's dolls, tattoos and body piercings have never been more popular in America. Academic researcher Anne Velliquette observes, "Today's social climate welcomes body art to an extent that no other period in modern history can rival." She maintains that tattoos can provide meaning to persons bewildered by the fragmentation and chaos of postmodern society:

> Your body is the one thing you have ultimate control over. Tattoos are a way of committing to something permanent and stable, of recording who and what you are right now. . . . The traditional stereotype is gone.

The stereotype Velliquette refers to has long relegated tattooing to marginal subgroups of society. Throughout the nineteenth and the early twentieth centuries, tattoos were associated with crusty sailors, hard-muscled prison inmates, leather-clad motorcycle gangs, or freak-show exhibits. As late as the mid–twentieth century, the practice remained limited to a highly specific demographic. UCLA professor Arnold Rubin elaborates on the typical tattooed person of the era:

> Clients were predominantly male, relatively young, artistically uninformed or conservative, and typically blue-collar. Their first exposure to the medium was usually a nonprofessional homemade tattoo associated with military, marginal, or institutionalized (primarily prison) subcultures.

Tattoo parlors were largely confined to back alleys and seedy, out-of-the-way streets. Surrounded by negative lore, the practice was viewed as taboo by mainstream society.

## Laying the Groundwork for Change

The fringe social movements that arose after World War II laid the groundwork for the modern rise in the popularity of tattoos. As writer Mecca Shakoor explains,

The Beatniks of the bohemian 1950s, with their interest in Asian philosophy and art, forged a crossover link between the blue-collar tradition of masculine tattoos to an increasingly spiritual and mystical body aesthetic practiced by both sexes during the Hippie movement of the 1960s.

Body art became but another radical form of expression in an array that included psychedelic drugs, open sex, and avant-garde music and art.

Nurtured by the more liberal attitudes of the 1960s and early 1970s, a new wave of tattoo artists began to break away from the overutilized "stock" patterns that had previously dominated the tattoo market. By developing highly artistic and individualized designs, such tattoo icons as Lyle Tuttle and Sailor Jerry shepherded the art along a radical new path. Researcher Hoag Levins writes:

> By 1972 a new, "modern" tattoo art scene surfaced across the U.S. as an expanding group of artists combined fine art disciplines with fantasy motifs executed in the lush, highly detailed tattooing style of the Japanese. The results were tattoos that were more like rich bits of tapestry than the stark pen scratchings that had characterized U.S. tattoo art of the World War II era.

During this period, Rubin contends, "the nature and practice of tattoo in the United States [changed] so dramatically the term 'renaissance' is justified."

## Piercing Popularity Comes Later

Body piercing has been even more taboo than tattooing in the United States, as many people still associate the practice with sadomasochism or other marginal behaviors. Even ear piercing, which has customarily been practiced by women, remained for men the stereotypical trademark of movie pirates and pimps well into the 1960s. A few audacious men, however, began to experiment with ear piercings during the beatnik and hippie movements of the 1950s and 1960s, laying the seeds for a growing acceptance of body piercing. In the 1970s, body piercing experienced somewhat of a genesis in the homosexual culture of California, but it remained a mostly underground activity.

The punk movement that sprung up in the late 1970s, however, very publicly embraced body piercing. Mecca Shakoor notes that "the next wave of . . . body ornamentation began with the rise of the punk movement in the 1970s and 1980s, in forms . . . overtly grim, political, and rebellious in expressive intent." Piercings were but one part of the punk ensemble—which often included stark black clothing, spiked leather belts, and outrageous hairstyles—intended openly to mock and shock mainstream society.

Although pierced punkers were certainly visible, they were still regarded as fringe elements by mainstream society. It took an influential underground book published in the late 1980s to really launch body piercing into the limelight. Journalist Dewey Webb explains:

> As near as anyone can tell, the current pincushion movement was triggered by *Modern Primitives*, a trade paperback that first appeared in record stores and esoteric bookshops in 1989. . . . Subtitled *An Investigation of Contemporary Adornment and Ritual*, the tome features interviews with two dozen body-modification enthusiasts, including bod-mod superstars like Fakir Musafar (a Silicon Valley ad exec whose anatomical accomplishments include dangling 24 one-pound weights from his chest with fishhooks) and octogenarian "Sailor Sid" Diller (the legendary, punked-out Popeye who delighted in setting off airport metal detectors with 54 genital piercings reportedly weighing in at a total of a pound and a half).

The book sold sixty-thousand copies over the next four years and provided body piercing with the necessary toehold from which it would gain mainstream popularity.

## Stars Carry the Banner

Celebrities have played a major role in helping tattoos and body piercings to gain popular acceptance. In the 1980s, pop icons such as Prince and Madonna began to sport tattoos openly. The trend grew and by the 1990s a myriad of movie stars, singers, and sports figures were displaying tattoos. The influence of tattooed and pierced celebrities on the general public has been profound, asserts Vince Hemingson, who produces a website featuring a variety of celebrity tattoos:

The fact that a generation of movie stars is getting tattoos is helping to erase the stigma attached to them as a lower-class thing. . . . These are the pop cultural icons of this age, and they have extraordinary influence.

Teenagers are perhaps the most susceptible to the sway of body-modified stars. Writer Joy Bennett Kinnon remarks, "Popular entertainers such as . . . Janet Jackson [and] Lenny Kravitz . . . have made piercing socially acceptable to their teen audience who are especially drawn to 'body art.'"

Fashion designers have not hesitated to jump on the body modification bandwagon. In the 1990s, both Calvin Klein and Jean-Paul Gaultier introduced piercing accessories to some of their garments. Again, the effect on the general public has been significant. "Pierced models relay a message to society that body piercing has become fashionable, which leads consumers to follow the fad and pierce themselves," notes writer Karen Robinson.

Sports fans can attest to the inroads tattoos and body piercings have made into popular culture. Basketball star Michael Jordan has long worn an earring, and his former teammate Dennis Rodman proudly sports multiple piercings and tattoos. Indeed, a 1997 Associated Press survey of National Basketball Association players found that over 35 percent had tattoos. "Professional sports observers estimate that similar percentages of America's national league football, hockey, and baseball players also have tattoos," notes Hoag Levins. Commenting on the cultural significance of these body-modified sports figures, Levins writes:

> Aside from raising the visibility of tattoos, these legions of sports figures—who also constitute one of the country's largest groups of millionaires—have had a major impact on the nature of the tattoo business. Much like millionaires, rock singers, movie stars and fashion models, they have created a new market for high-end custom tattoo art studios geared to an affluent and demanding clientele.

## Current Popularity

At the dawn of the twenty-first century, society's attraction to body ornamentation has moved beyond a mere faddish fascination with celebrity. Journalist Danny Tenkham explains: "Decorating one's body has never seemed so chic. Tattoos are becoming the rule more than the exception and are displayed on many different body parts by all types of people." The current statistics illustrate the practice's popularity. Writer Corrine Gibbons reports that 3 to 5 percent of the populations of Western societies now sport at least one tattoo, with more than half considering one. The Alliance of Professional Tattoo Artists estimates the percentage at a much higher one in ten. Tattoos are even more popular within certain subgroups: Gibbons notes that more than one-third of the soldiers in the U.S. Army are tattooed, with 22 percent having three or more.

Approximately ten percent of teenagers now wear tattoos. Danny Tenkham observes that "college age kids have accepted the trend more than anyone. Exhibiting art on their bodies has practically become a cultural rite to distancing themselves from their parents." Indeed, a 2001 survey of college students conducted by the medical journal *Mayo Clinic Proceedings* found that more than half of those interviewed had a body piercing. Signaling a shift from the once male-dominated practice of tattooing, women now outnumber men among college students who display body art.

## Baby Boomers and Soccer Moms

Although youths constitute the majority of the body modification market, the demographics of body modifiers are broadening. In the course of her research, Velliquette discovered that "all types of individuals are getting tattoos right now." She writes:

> I've interviewed doctors, lawyers, teachers, college students, housewives, on and on. It's a very diverse sub-culture. . . .We used to associate tattoos with criminals, bikers, sailors, all sorts of social deviants. That's not the case anymore.

Arnold Rubin adds, "Major demographic shifts have brought in a greater number of females and generally older, better educated, more affluent, and more artistically sophisticated clients."

Even baby boomers have begun to embrace body art. Karen Robinson argues that parents who sport them are often trying to reclaim their radical pasts:

As baby boomers realized they are becoming their conservative parents, body piercing helps them recapture their youthful days of . . . rebellion during the late '60's and '70's. For baby boomers, body piercing symbolizes their refusal to become full-fledged members of the conservative world.

Unlike many celebrities, however, these more conservative body art aficionados are usually clandestine in their participation. Robinson continues:

Often, baby boomers have nipples, navels, or even genitalia pierced rather than eyebrows, tongues, or cheeks . . . because the former types are easily hidden by clothing. As they cover a nipple-ring with an Armani business suit, baby boomers maintain a conservative, business-like appearance while having the satisfaction of secretly breaking social norms.

Perhaps the most surprising group demonstrating an affinity for body modification is suburban women. In November 1997, reporter Lauren Donovan of North Dakota's *Bismarck Tribune* found that the fastest growing demographic in the local tattoo market was 30- to 40-year old "soccer moms." By no means fringe individuals, these women were firmly ensconced in family, community, and church relationships. The medical journal *Physician Assistant* estimates that tattooing quadrupled among women in the last two decades of the twentieth century, with women now constituting half of all tattoo devotees.

## A Booming Business

As tattoos and body piercings have grown in popularity, the business of body modification has exploded. Corrine Gibbons reports that "in the U.S., tattooing was the sixth fastest growing retail business in 1996, after the Internet, paging services, bagel stores, computer retail outlets, and cellular phone stores." The escalating interest in body art is evidenced by a growing curiosity among the general public; in 2001, notes Ann Oldenburg, "tattoos [were] the third-most-requested search item on the Internet search engine Lycos, right behind Dragonball and Britney Spears."

Capitalizing on the public's growing fascination with tattoos and body piercings, marketers are pushing body art into heretofore-unexplored territory. Writer Allison Hogge explains:

> Tattoos have become so mainstream that they're beginning
> to show up in unusual places, like the toy market. Tattoos
> aren't just popping up on the bodies of young women.
> They're popping up on the most famous of all young
> women: Barbie.

"This is the ultimate proof of how widely skin art is accepted,"
says Anne Velliquette, referring to Tattoo Fun Skipper, a doll
that comes with tattoo stickers of flowers and peace signs. The
marketing of body art to children has been so effective, asserts
Myrna Armstrong, a professor at the Texas Tech Health Sci-
ences Center School of Nursing, that "children today see tattoos almost as toys because of the popularity of temporary
rub-on tattoos and dolls children can tattoo with markers."

For adults, the skin has become but another place to display
symbols of brand affiliation and loyalty. An informal survey of
West Coast tattoo parlors conducted by the International
Trademark Association (INTA) found that the Harley-Davidson
logo was the most widely requested trademark tattoo. In the
New York area, the Yankees baseball team logo, Chevy Camaro,
and Nike swoosh are the most popular. According to the INTA:

> Tattooed trademarks are more than symbols of extreme
> brand loyalty. It seems that the trademarks that are the most
> frequently seen as tattoos tend to be those that have
> achieved a certain cultural impact; ones that have become,
> for their admirers, a way of life. Those that wear tattoos as
> trademarks appear to wear them as a kind of cultural source
> indicator to show their membership to a particular group.

## Exploring the Cultural Significance of Body Modification

Tattoos have now entered the vaulted realms of academic sym-
posiums, museum exhibits, and theater productions. They are
being celebrated for both their artistic and historical significance, and a similar exploration of body piercing is probably
not far behind.

The following chapters of *Examining Pop Culture: Body*

*Piercing and Tattoos* further examine the phenomenon of body modification. Chapter One, The History of Body Modification, traces the roots of body art—from ancient times until the golden age of tattooing in the first half of the twentieth century. In Chapter Two, The Basics of Tattoos and Body Piercings, writers explain the procedures and perils of various body modification practices. Chapter Three, The Psychology of Body Modification, explores the personal and sociological significance of tattoos and body piercings. Finally, Chapter Four, The Controversial Nature of Body Art, assembles viewpoints on such contentious issues as body art and business attire, the interpretation and removal of gang tattoos, and parental involvement in youths' body modifications.

EXAMINING POP CULTURE

# The History of Body Modification

# Tattoos in Ancient Times

Georgina Wiman-Rudzinski

In the following excerpt, writer Georgina Wiman-Rudzinski traces the rich history of ancient tattooing. Wiman-Rudzinski reports that the first evidence of tattooing dates to the body of a prehistoric man uncovered in the ice of the Italian Alps in 1991. Carbon dating proved that the man died approximately thirty-three hundred years before the birth of Christ.

Moving around the globe from Egypt to Polynesia, the author goes on to explain the mythologies and customs that surrounded tattoos in a variety of ancient cultures. A teacher's assistant and writer living in Canada, Wiman-Rudzinski has written articles on both tattooing and body piercing.

TATTOOS HAVE EXISTED SINCE LONG BEFORE THE birth of Jesus Christ. The earliest evidence of tattoos was found on the now famous Iceman that was found in the Otzal Alps between Austria and Italy in 1991. Carbon 14 dating done on the bones and tissue of the Iceman proved that he had died some 5,300 years ago (3,300 B.C.). Professor Konrad Spindler of the Innsbruck University speculated that the blue tattoos adorning the skin of the Iceman were simply ornamental, were for magical purposes, or perhaps they were used to indicate his social status among his group or tribe. They may also have been done to relieve pain or ailments that he suffered from or to keep him from getting sick. Why the tattoos were done is not clear but the fact that he was extraordi-

Excerpted from "The History of Tattoos: Before the Birth of Christ," by Georgina Wiman-Rudzinski, www.pagewise.com, 2001. Copyright © 2001 by PageWise, Inc. Reprinted with permission.

narily well preserved after spending 5,300 years under ice gave the professionals that studied the body the unique opportunity to identify the images that graced his skin. In all, he had a total of 58 tattoos that were likely done with charcoal and were mostly made up of simple dots and lines. Coincidentally, he also had an earring.

## Tattooing in Ancient Egypt and Libya

Tattooing was also a custom in Egypt during the Third and Fourth Dynasties (2686–2493 B.C.) while the pyramids of Gizeh were being built. Evidence found in archaeological and anthropological digs suggests that the Egyptians had already started the process of tattooing with needles by that point. The clay dolls that the children played with at the time were also adorned with tattoo-like designs and they further served to prove that tattooing was alive during this time.

Another tattooed Egyptian of note was Amunet, who was

# The Religious Significance of Tattoos in Ancient Societies

Among the best-preserved mummies is that of a woman from Thebes from Dynasty XI (2160–1994 B.C.), whose tomb identifies her as Amunet, Priestess of Hathor. . . . Tattoo patterns remain clearly visible on her flesh. . . . She bore parallel lines on her arms and thighs and an elliptical pattern below the navel in the pelvic region.

Several other female mummies from this period also clearly show similar tattoos as well as ornamental scarring (cicatrization, still popular in parts of Africa) across the lower abdomen. The tattoos are all seemingly abstract: a series of dots, dashes and lozenges and for this reason they are often dismissed as random and meaningless. . . . Those dots and dashes, so abstract to the non-initiated, actually hold protective and fertility-promoting significance. The lozenges are anciently and traditionally connected to the a priestess of the goddess Hathor at Thebes during the Eleventh Dynasty (2160–1994 B.C.). Amunet's mummy was very well preserved and had parallel lines tattooed on the arms and thighs as well as an elliptical design below her navel. Statuettes decorated with designs similar to the ones found on Amunet were buried with male mummies and were supposed to arouse the sexual instincts of the dead fellow and ensure his resurrection. Egyptologists feel that the statuettes, called "brides of the dead," were symbols of fertility and rejuvenation. When the Egyptians passed on their culture the art of tattoos traveled with them to Crete, Greece, Persia and Arabia.

In Libya (which is quite close to Egypt), male and female mummies with tattoos have been discovered. Some of the male mummies were tattooed with sun worshipping images. . . . The mummies that were found in the tomb of Seti I (dating from about 1300 B.C.) were tattooed with pictures symbolizing a fierce goddess named Neith, who led warriors into battle.

primal female power of the universe, the Great Mother, so appropriate for a priestess of Hathor.

Why do people get tattooed anyway? Modern individuals may do it for all sorts of reasons, trivial or profound, but ancient and traditional societies possess serious and conscious reasoning.

The traditional reasons for tattooing include:
• to connect with the Divine.
• as a tribute or act of sacrifice to a deity.
• as a talisman, a permanent amulet that cannot be lost, to provide magical or medical protection.

Many traditional cultures also use tattoos on the flesh as a sort of *passport* to the world after death, although interestingly, with all the emphasis on the next world in ancient Egyptian culture, there is no indication that this was the case there.

"Tattoos in Ancient Egypt," *Tour Egypt Monthly*, December 11, 2000. www. egyptmonth.com.

Tattoo needles used during the Bronze Age (about 200–500 B.C.) are on display in Bornholm's Museum in Røne, Denmark.

## Early Polynesian Tattoos

The Polynesians were very artistic and used elaborate geometrical designs in the tattoos that they did as far back as 1200 B.C. The Lapitas used flat, chisel-shaped pieces of bone that were roughly two to four centimeters long and were sharpened at one end and resembled a comb. The instrument was dipped in pigment which was made of water and soot and the instrument was then hit with a small mallet to drive the pigment into the skin. The Lapitas took their tattoos very seriously and started with a design on one area of the body and then continued the design until their bodies were entirely covered with tattoos. . . . The Lapita people were also very skilled potters and showed their love for tattoos on the pottery that they made. The Lapita colonized the Solomons, Hebrides, Figi, Tonga and Samoa where the art of tattooing was continued.

## The Development of Tattoos in Europe

Anthropologist Sergei Ivanovich Rudenko discovered the next part of the puzzle in 1948. He discovered a Pazyryk chief who had been mummified and was extremely well preserved. The Pazyryks were powerful iron age horsemen and warriors who lived in Eastern Europe and Western Asia from 600 to 200 B.C. The chief was approximately 50 years old at the time of his death and was heavily tattooed with interlocking designs which were primarily made up of beasts. His chest was adorned with griffins. His right arm had tattoos of a donkey, a mountain ram, two deer and another unidentified carnivore while his left arm was tattooed with two deer and a mountain goat. The chief's suit of decoration continued on his right leg which featured a fish from his foot to his knee on the front and a monster and four rams in a design on the remaining part of his right leg. His left leg was also tattooed but the design was indistinguishable since it was not as well preserved as the rest of his body. His back was also tattooed with small circles along his vertebrae which were likely done for therapeutic reasons to relieve some sort of pain that the chief had been having. The Pazyryk tombs that Rudenko discovered were very well preserved and contained skeletons and intact bodies of horses and embalmed humans as well as a wealth of artifacts. . . . There were also fabrics from Persia and China found in the tomb which indicated that the Pazyryks had traveled to those areas of the world.

In 1993, another Pazyryk mummy was discovered, but this time it was a female. She was buried in a larch tree casket that had deer and snow leopards carved into it. She was tattooed

*Some cultures use tattooing as a way to identify certain groups within their village.*

with creatures similar to those found on the chief. She had been tattooed approximately 2,400 [years] (400 B.C.) before she was found. This mummy was discovered in the Umak plateau in Siberia by an archaeologist named Natalya Polasmak who said "We wouldn't be as happy if we had found solid gold." Gilded ornaments, dishes, a brush, a pot containing marijuana, and a hand mirror of polished metal were also found in the tomb. It is believed that the Pazyryks tattooed animals on themselves for magic, totemism and to absorb the character of the animals that they had tattooed on them. It is believed that the female mummy was therefore tattooed with the rams, deer, fish and griffins as a way of honouring them and/or adopting the qualities that made these animals exceptional—ferocity, quickness, cunning, etc. The discovery of the second mummy also made it clear that in the Pazyryk culture, both men and women who had established a certain class or stature in the group, were allowed to be tattooed.

## Nubian and Scythian Tattoos

Nubian mummies dating back from about 400 B.C. (the same time as the Pazyryks) had the Egyptian god of revelry (Bes) tattooed on them. Bes also served as the patron god of music and dancing girls and had the distinction of being the master of ceremonies at orgies. He was portrayed in Egyptian works of art as an ape-like dwarf who wore an animal skin. It would seem that Egyptian gods were popular icons to tattoo on yourself during that period of time as the likeness of other gods (such as the Egyptian sun god, Ra) have also been found on mummies that have been discovered to this point.

The Scythians died out close to the time of Jesus' birth (2 B.C.). They were victims of intermarriage and conquest and died out as a result. Archaeologists found a royal tomb, which contained the skeletons of a prince, a princess and an infant outside the town of Ordzhonikidze in the southern Ukraine in 1920. Just after the Second World War, archaeologists found a well preserved Scythian chief with some fantastic tattoos in the Altai Mountains of Southern Siberia. The chief's tattoos represented different totems and game animals. They were done in a very distinct style, which was repeated in their wood carvings, leather, jewelry, embroidery, weaving, and other art forms.

# Body Piercing History and Anthropology

Raven Rowanchilde

In the following selection, writer Raven Rowanchilde traces various types of body piercings from their ancient roots to their modern popularity. Rowanchilde writes that the piercing of certain body parts, such as the ear, developed from relatively benign cultural myths and rituals, while others, such as the foreskin of the penis, evolved from mere practical contrivances into adornments. Rowanchilde is cofounder of the Urban Primitive Design Studio, a body art establishment in Toronto, Canada.

EAR PIERCINGS ARE THE MOST WIDELY PRACticed piercings among cultural groups in Africa, India, Indonesia, and North and South America. Pre-industrial societies ritualized ear piercing to mark the life stages of an individual and to signify group affiliation. Ear cartilage piercings, especially popular among the Masai and Fulani, also emphasized beauty and wealth. Stretched earlobes predominate among groups in Indonesia and South America. Stretched earlobes have increased in popularity among modern devotees. Earlobe piercings constitute the most socially acceptable form of body piercing in industrialized countries. Modern ear adornments include the conch, the tragus, and two innovative cartilage piercings, the daith and the rook, introduced by California body piercer Erik Dakota.

∎

# Facial and Upper Body Piercings

Nostril, lip and septum piercings occur as part of rituals marking the passage from childhood to adulthood in many societies of Africa, India, South America, Indonesia, New Guinea, Australia and the Pacific. Septum piercings tend mostly to be found on men and nostril piercings on women. Myths of Aboriginal groups in Central Australia note the existence of legendary female warriors, the Alknarintja, who wore bones in their septums and wielded men's sacred objects. Eyebrow, nasion, madison and navel piercings are unique to modern Western societies. The "father of modern piercing," Doug Malloy, apparently introduced the folklore that ancient Egyptians pierced their navels as a sign of royalty. There is no evidence to support this statement. Hans Peter Duerr reports evidence of nipple piercing in the 14th century. Queen Isabella of Bavaria introduced a fashion of dress that opened the neckline to the navel. According to Duerr, "This fashion eventually led to the application of rouge to freely displayed nipples . . . to placing diamond studded rings on caps on them, even to piercing them and passing gold chains through them decorated with diamonds, possibly to demonstrate the youthful resilience of the bosom."

Folklore about male nipple piercing emphasizes themes of masculinity and status. According to Doug Malloy, "The proud Roman centurions . . . wore nipple rings as a sign of virility and courage and as a dress accessory for holding their short capes." Another variation involving Teutonic warriors also circulates.

Modern motivations behind facial and upper body piercings include: fashion trend, aesthetic or erotic appeal, shock value, sensual enhancement and group affiliation. Nipple piercings are usually horizontal but they may be vertical in some cases. Wearers of facial piercings or visible upper body piercings in modern industrialized societies may suffer social stigmatization, loss of employment, loss of family support, violence and other forms of discrimination. . . .

# Oral Piercings

Nostril, septum and labret [beneath the lip] piercings are most widely practiced among cultural groups in New Guinea, Africa, India, Southeast Asia, Australia, and North and South

America. Different cultural groups in West Africa, North America and the Amazon wear large lip plugs in their stretched labret piercings. These piercings and subsequent stretchings mark the passage from childhood to adulthood and signify group affiliation. Large lip plugs also emphasize the importance of oratory skills among the Suya of South America. The stretched upper labret piercing is unique to cultural groups in Chad.

Tongue, lip, upper lip, and cheek piercings are unique to modern Western societies. Modern labret piercings are smaller and more discrete. Upper lip piercings mimic beauty marks and bear the names of Hollywood icons, [such as] Madonna and Marilyn Monroe. Tongue frenulums, uvula piercings and upper lip frenulums highlight the Western obsession with individuality at any cost. Unfortunately, these piercings often result in costly dental repairs and have a high rate of tearing and/or rejection.

The only evidence of tongue piercing in the anthropological literature concerns the ancient Maya of Mexico and Central America. Maya royalty practiced temporary tongue piercings to commune with the spirits of their ancestors during special rituals. Tongue scarification (cutting and branding) was practiced during mourning rites among Aboriginal groups in Central Australia. Similarly, pre-contact Hawaiians tattooed their tongues as part of mourning ceremonies.

Motivations behind modern oral piercings include: fashion trend, aesthetic appeal, shock value, group affiliation and sensual enhancement (especially with tongue piercings). As with facial piercings, wearers of oral piercings in modern industrialized societies may suffer social stigmatization, loss of employment, loss of family support, violence and other forms of discrimination.

# Male Genital Piercings

To reinforce male identification, many cultures subject their male children to various forms of painful male genital modification (MGM). MGMs such as circumcision, piercing, penis inserts and various forms of penile incision establish sexual identity and, through the stoic endurance of pain, elevate the status of the individual from boy to man. Male initiation rituals, a requirement in all primitive societies, unequivocally establish a man's value in his society. The most prolific form of male genital modification is circumcision, the removal of the foreskin to expose the glans of the penis. Primitive societies perform circumcision on young boys usually from ages eight to fifteen as an essential part of initiation rituals into manhood. With the exception of the bris [ritual circumcision] performed by Jewish Mohels [religious performers of circumcision], no religious ritual attends infant circumcision. Physicians in modern societies routinely perform circumcision on uninformed, unprepared and non-consenting infant boys for "hygienic" reasons. Modern MGM enthusiasts get pierced primarily for erotic reasons.

## Types of Male Genital Piercings

Foreskin: Believed to have evolved from a practice that originated in ancient Greece . . . during the Olympic Games. Greek athletes competed in the nude. To prevent their genitals from flapping around and reduce risk of chafing and tearing, the athletes fastened a ribbon around the foreskin and tied the ends securely at the base of the penis. . . . The practice evolved into a permanent form in Rome [between] 200 to 400 C.E. The Romans pierced the prepuce [foreskin] of athletes and slaves with a metal ring that they welded shut. The Romans called this device a fibula. It's function was to prevent erections—not for protection but to ensure the athlete didn't break training and the slaves didn't procreate.

Dydoe: Southeast Asia, India; penetrates the glans [tip of the penis] along the coronal ridge. Said to enhance pleasure in women and to increase sensitivity in circumcised men.

Hafada: Pierced through the skin of the scrotum, usually on one side. Arabian origins—traditionally performed at puberty to mark passage into manhood. Soldiers in the French Foreign Legion possibly introduced the hafada to Europe. . . .

## Female Genital Piercing

With the exception of inner labia piercings, all female genital piercings are modern inventions. . . . Motivations behind female genital piercings include: fashion trend, aesthetic appeal, shock value, sensual enhancement, sexual reclamation and erotic attraction.

References to female genital modification in the anthropological literature also highlight sexual attraction in a number of different forms. For example, Trukese women of Polynesia pierced their labia and hung little bells from them to attract suitors. Hottentot women of South Africa stretched their labia minora forming little "skirts" or "aprons" because Hottentot men regarded women with elongated labia as better lovers.

Female genital modification also has a parallel history as a means of enforcing sexual control. Female circumcision is practiced on young girls, usually between the ages of four and eight. Cultural groups in the Sudan, Somalia, other parts of Africa, the Arabian Peninsula, and parts of Asia and South America circumcise their young girls to establish permanent sex roles and enforce chastity. The World Health Organization (WHO) estimates that 114 million girls and women have been circumcised. Female circumcision ranges from the partial or total removal of the clitoris to pharaonic infibulation, which involves excision of the clitoris and the inner and outer labia and the sewing up of the vulva, leaving only a 2 or 3 cm hole to allow urine and menstrual blood to pass. The surgery is usually performed by the local midwife, who uses either a knife, razor, scissors or broken glass to remove the genital tissue and acacia thorns to sew up what remains, often without the use of any sterilization procedures or anesthetic. The fundamental difference between male genital modification (MGM) and female genital mutilation (FGM) is that the former enhances sexual pleasure while the latter eliminates it. In addition to robbing women of sexual pleasure, female circumcision causes emotional trauma and tremendous health problems that range from tetanus, urinary tract infections, chronic disability or even death. North Americans have a similar history of using genital modification to enforce sexual control. In addition to bedtime bondage devices and enemas, physicians in North America in the early 1900s routinely circumcised young boys and performed clitoridectomies on girls to discourage masturbation.

# Modern Efforts to Eradicate Female Genital Mutilation

Today, largely due to the efforts of the World Health Organization, educated women in countries that circumcise young girls are lobbying to abolish the practice. But cultural practices that have been rigidly enforced for centuries do not change overnight. These women face a great deal of resistance not only from the larger culture, but also from young girls who want to be circumcised so that they will not be stigmatized or excluded, because infibulation is considered a requirement for marriage. Some women opt to have their daughters' clitorises temporarily pierced to satisfy the cultural requirement of bloodshed. The problem with the temporary piercing is that there is no permanent marker of "proof" that the individual endured the prescribed cultural ordeal.

Another possibility remains: Female genital piercing performed in a professional, safe and hygienic manner could satisfy . . . the cultural requirement of pain, bloodshed and the need for a physical marker. Best of all, female genital piercings done properly, enhance female pleasure.

# Early European Encounters with Polynesian Tattoos

R.W.B. Scutt and Christopher Gotch

Although there is evidence of tattooing in ancient Europe, the tattoos of modern Western society did not evolve directly from European roots. Rather, the artistic forms were imported by sailors returning from expeditions to the Polynesian islands of the South Pacific in the late 1700s and early 1800s.

During his service as a registered nurse in the British Royal Navy, Surgeon Captain R.W.B. Scutt has seen tens of thousands of modern tattooed sailors. In his book *Art, Sex, and Symbol: The Mystery of Tattooing*, Scutt seeks to clarify the myths and legends that surround the experiences of these sailors' forefathers, the early explorers of the South Pacific who first encountered the tattooed natives of the Polynesian islands.

THE YEAR 1769 AND CAPTAIN JAMES COOK CAN BE hailed as concomitant factors vital to the history of tattooing. It was in this year [during his explorations of the Polynesian islands of the Pacific] that Cook and his crew came into contact with tattooing on a scale never before seen by Western eyes.

## A Scrupulous Observer

Through [Joseph Banks, naturalist and historian to Cook's ship, the *Endeavour*] we learn how it all began. So informative is he, so

■

invaluable his observation, so pithy his style it is worth having his detailed account first hand, for one can almost feel the sharp prick of the instrument as it is tapped smartly into the skin.

> I shall now mention their methods of painting their bodies, or tattow as it is called in their language. This they do by inlaying black under their skin in such a manner as to be indelible. Everyone is thus marked in different parts of his body according to his humour or different circumstances of his life. Some have ill-designed figures of men, birds or dogs; but they more generally have a Z, either plain (as is generally the case with the women, on every joint of their fingers and toes and often round the outside of their feet) or in different figures such as squares, circles, crescents etc. which both sexes have on their arms and legs; in short, they have an infinite diversity of figures in which they place this mark.

What significance these marks had, Banks never discovered; nor did he see more than a single instance of facial tattooing. He noticed, however, several old men almost wholly marked with patches of black, parts of which appeared to have been the result of a form of branding, so deep were the indentations, but he was told that these men were from the island of Noonoora.

> Although they vary so much in the application of the figures . . . all the islanders I have seen (except those of Oheteroa) agree in having their buttocks covered with a deep black. Over this most have arches which are often a quarter of an inch broad, drawn one above the other as high as their short ribs, and neatly worked on their edges with indentations etc. These arches are their great pride; both men and women show them with great pleasure, whether as a mark of beauty, or a proof of their perseverance and resolution in bearing pain I cannot tell. The pain in doing this is almost intolerable, specially the arches upon the loins, which are so much more susceptible to pain than the fleshy buttocks.

On a later voyage John Gore (First Lieutenant of H.M.S *Resolution*) noted that

> The people of Atiu are . . . like those of Otaheite, differing in nothing that I know of except their artificial colouring.

Those have Black Arses, and these have Black Bellies Privities included and Black legs reaching to Just above their Calf . . . Their women have only Black Leggs.

Apparently lamp-black prepared from the smoke of an oily nut was used and kept in coconut shells, 'and occasionally mixed with water for use'. Flat bone or shell, the lower part of which was serrated to form from three to twenty teeth, was used depending upon the stage of operation. Bound to a handle, this implement was dipped into 'the blak liquer' and, by a sharp tap on the handle, pierced the skin producing some blood. Banks

saw this operation performed . . . on the buttocks of a girl about 14 years of age; for some time she bore it with great resolution, but afterwards began to complain, and to a little time grew so outrageous that all the threats and force her friends could use could hardly oblige her to endure it. I had occasion to remain in an adjoining house at least after this operation began, and yet went away before it was finished, in which time only one side was black, the other having been done some weeks before.

Banks was mystified by whatever induced these people to suffer so much pain, for the marking was common to all, being performed between the ages of fourteen and eighteen.

# The Art of Moko

After the South Sea Islands, visited in August 1769, Cook's *Endeavour* reached North Island, New Zealand, and it was here in October of the same year that the tattooing art known as Moko or Amoca was first discovered. [Banks writes:]

The people were in general of a middling size, though there was no one who measured more than six feet. Their colour was a dark brown. Their lips were stained with something put under the skin (as in the Otahite tattow) and their faces marked with deeply engraved furrows also coloured black and formed in regular spirals. Of these, the oldest people had much the greatest quantity and most deeply channelled, in some not less than one-sixteenth part of an inch. . . . The faces of some were painted with a red colour in oil, some all over, others in part only. . . . A few had on their faces or arms regular scars as if made with a sharp instrument, such as I have seen on the faces of negroes.

In November 1769, the ship arrived at Opoorage, near Auckland. Here, Banks noticed that 'Amoca or black stains' was even more universal. The broad spiral on each buttock was common also, often combined with lines around the thighs to give an effect of 'striped breeches', yet customs varied between tribes, some demanding considerable coverage, others merely a spot on the lip. 'One of the old men . . . showed us the instrument with which they stain their bodies; it was exactly like that used at Otahite'.

## Noting the Nuances

Whilst women seemed content to stain their lips black, with only an occasional patch of black elsewhere, the men appeared to enlarge their collection of markings annually. Indeed, 'the elders were almost covered with it'. To Banks, their faces were the most remarkable, being furrowed with lines both deep and broad to make them more ferocious in aspect for warfare.

> Yet ugly as it certainly looks, it is impossible to avoid admiring the extreme elegance and justness of the figures traced, which on the face always different spirals, and upon the body generally different figures, resembling somewhat the foliages of old chasing upon gold and silver.

> All these are finished with a masterly taste and execution, for, of a hundred which at first sight would be judged to be exactly the same, no two on close examination prove alike. . . . Their wild imagination scorns to copy, as appears in almost all their works.

He noted that the degree of 'Amoca' varied along the coast but that facial spirals were common throughout, and he arrived at the conclusion that it increased in ratio to population; yet '. . . the buttocks, which in the islands were the principal seat of this ornament, in general escape untouched'.

He noticed too that besides 'this dying in grain' the natives painted themselves with red ochre, this being practised particularly by women. 'If any of us', he commenced, 'had unthinkingly ravished a kiss from one of these savages, our transgressions were written in most legible characters on our noses, which our companions could not fail to see on our first interview'.

## The Primitive Technique of Tattoo

Sidney Parkinson's drawings, in *A Journal of a Voyage to the South Seas . . .* , show 'their tataowing instruments' which he describes in rather greater detail than Banks, perhaps because, having actually undergone the operation himself, he had more time to study the technique at close quarters.

> The handles . . . are wood; towards the end of which is a hollow made to lay the forefinger of the hand which holds it: the head is made of one or two flat pieces of bone of various breadths tapering to a point towards the handle, to which it is fastened very tight with fibres of the bark of a tree: the broad part, or bottom, is cut into many small sharp teeth. When they mark any person, they dip the instrument, a small one or large one, according to the figure intended, into a black liquid, or juice, expressed from some plant, and, placing it upon the part intended to be marked, give it a small blow with the paddle, which causes a great deal of pain. These instruments are about five inches in length . . . the paddle made of wood . . . neatly shaped and worked very smooth . . . is about eighteen inches long.

Parkinson, hardly a naturalist of the calibre of Banks, sounds unsure about the black liquid 'expressed from some plant', but earlier in the narrative he describes 'E Tootooe' (*Telopoea perspicua*), the fruit of which tree 'is a sort of nut, which yields a very fat kernel, of which they make their black dye, used in tataowing, by burning them and receiving the smoke'.

## Coining the Term "Tattoo"

Apparently it was Cook himself who introduced the word 'tattoo' into the English language, as a variation of *tattow*, *tatau*, or *tattaw*, all derived from *ta*, the Polynesian word for knocking or striking. It is possible, therefore, that the word is onomatopoeic in origin, representing the 'tat-tat' sound made by hitting the tattooing tool. However, some authorities do not accept this derivation, but consider that the word originated from the Javanese language where *tau* means 'a wound, scar'.

The word 'tattoo' ('taptoo', or 'taptoe') had been used since 1644 to denote the beating of drums *(Shorter Oxford English Dictionary)*. The word 'tattooing' has incidentally been adopted with only comparatively minor variation into many European languages (German: *Tatowirung*; French: *tatouage*; Italian: *tatuaggio*; Danish: *tatoveringer)*.

Both Cook and Banks returned to the South Pacific and in addition to providing further written material on the subject, actually brought home with them in 1774 a tattooed native called Omai, who was exhibited throughout the country. History does not reveal how he enjoyed the change of climate, but two years later Cook took him aboard the *Resolution* and returned him to his native island.

Banks seems to have made no attempt to discern the motives behind tattooing in the South Seas. He was obviously baffled by the apparent stupidity of the practice. 'Possibly superstition may have something to do with it; nothing else . . . could be a sufficient cause for apparently so absurd a custom'. Banks was told that some of the marks had 'significations', but what these were he never discovered.

## Possible Motives for the Practice

Whilst Banks faithfully relates his experiences in the South Seas and New Zealand, Tasman never mentioned tattooing at all in his report of his voyage to New Zealand in 1648 so it might be presumed not to have existed then. If this be so, it is extraordinary that so peculiar a custom could have developed within a century and a quarter. Yet from the drawings by Parkinson in the British Museum, the collection of Lindauer portraits in the Auckland City Art Gallery, and the preserved Maori heads in museums throughout the world this Amoco or Moko tattooing was a skilled art form. Its origin, particularly as facial decoration, remains obscure, but it was regarded by some as a development of battle paint. However, this is clearly not the sole explanation. A more convincing motive is that the marks rendered a sort of agelessness to the bearer, and also indicated the badge of distinction between chief and slave.

Replicas of the intricate patterns were used too as, or instead of, signatures, especially by chiefs, in legal documents. [Voyager J.S.] Polack mentioned the pride that the New

Zealanders took in adding Moko curvatures to their signatures: 'Our risibility has often been excited in viewing an aged chief, whose scant locks have weathered upwards of seventy winters, drawing with intense care his signature, with inclined head and extended tongue, as is the wont of young European practitioners in the art of penmanship'.

Some regard Moko as a complete analogy to European heraldry, but with the difference that whereas the coat of arms attested the merits of ancestors, the Moko illustrated the merits of the person decorated with it.

## Painted for War?

Conversely [General H.G.] Robley considered it to be a reflection of tribal character, in that the fierceness of the pattern corresponded to the fierceness of their nature. It may have been a custom arising from the need for a psychological boost in battle, the equivalent of Dutch courage, or similar to the Scots Highlander discarding his plaid for battle, so as to sport nakedness as a badge of courage.

Indeed Moko might well have been an extenuation of battle paint.

> The men were all stripped for action, but I also notice that the appearance of nakedness is completely taken away by the tattooing, and the colour of the skin, and the arms and equipment. . . . The men, in fact, look much better than when dressed in their Maori clothing. Every man almost without exception is covered with tattooing from the knees to the waist; the face is also covered with dark spiral lines.

Julien Crozet noted that the chiefs were delighted to show off their body tattooing. He commented that while the designs on the faces always varied, those on the buttocks were always the same, namely a neat spiral line of which the first or starting point was at the centre of the most fleshy part and then successively embraced the whole circumference. To have fine tattooed faces, he said, was the great ambition among men both to render themselves attractive to the ladies and conspicuous in war.

If killed by the enemy, the heads of the untattooed were treated with indignity, and kicked on one side, while those conspicuous by their beautiful Moko were carefully cut off, stuck on a pole and preserved; all of which was 'highly gratifying to the survivors and the spirits of their late possessor'.

Obviously to set off the Moko adequately, all facial hair had to be removed. Originally a pair of mussel shells was used for this purpose, but with the arrival of Europeans, large metal tweezers took their place, and could generally be seen hanging from the neck or attached to a piece of clothing. 'Whenever the gentleman could find no other employment he indefatigably occupied himself with them. To allow the beard to grow was regarded as a sign of old age and proof that the wearer had ceased to care for his appearance; a person with a beard was addressed as *E weki* which is a salutation equivalent to "old man"'. A man unmarked with Moko was regarded as a nobody and often called *papatea*, meaning 'plain-face'.

The very abstraction of pattern in Moko tattooing is what makes it so fascinating to us today. To Darwin however, unaccustomed to this form of art, Moko was the antithesis of beauty and he made clear his disapproval. He compared the New Zealander unfavourably with the Tahitian. . . .

## Tattoos' Significance to Women

With women Moko was restricted to the lips and chin. 'We really must just have a few lines on our lips, else when we grow old our lips will shrivel up and we shall be so very ugly'.

Any tattooing of other areas indicated rank, and in some cases chin tattoos denoted the married state, but torso marks were undoubtedly rare. [Observer J.C. Bidwill writes,] 'I used to think it very ornamental in the men, but what its use can be in a woman I cannot imagine, as they are always covered. . . . I have seen the arms and bodies of the New Zealand women so covered with these powerful blue marks that they looked as if they had on them a tight-fitting figured chintz dress'.

As the custom died out amongst the men the women clung on to this facial make-up, at least into the early part of the twentieth century. In 1896, General Robley recorded that 'many Maori women still decorate themselves and it suits them well'.

## Technique and Craft

The instruments used in Moko technique varied. Those somewhat like chisels and called Uhi had a sharp edge made from the bone of a bird's wing, a shark's teeth, stones, or hardwood, the average breadth of blade being 1/4 inch. The incision was made by applying the edge to the skin and driving it in by means of a sharp tap with a mallet called He Mahoe. If the tap was a little too heavy, the chisel sometimes went right through the cheek. The operation inevitably produced deep scarred furrows, which were so characteristic of the Moko described by early travellers. Later, sharper iron chisels were introduced from England, and the work became finer. Finally, pricking with needles replaced the cutting process and the operation developed into a sort of tattooing.

The pigment was invariably carbon, manufactured in a variety of curious ways, such as the burning of the resin of the Kauri pine, the Aweto Hotete (or vegetable caterpillar) or even gunpowder.

The pattern of lines, curves and spirals was very complex. [General Robley notes,] 'A complete fresco of elaborate Moko was a production . . . only of time. Months and even years passed in giving the artist or his successor full scope in the completion of his human pictures'.

Certain artists stood out above others. Earle, a draughtsman, travelling with Charles Darwin in the *Beagle* in 1827, mentions one called Aranghie:

The [tattoo artist] was considered by his countrymen a perfect master in the art of tattooing, and men of the highest rank and importance were in the habit of travelling long journeys in order to put their skin under his skilful hands. Indeed, so highly were his works esteemed that I have seen many of his drawings exhibited even after his death. A neighbour of mine very lately killed a chief who had been tattooed by Aranghie, and appreciating the artist's work so highly, he skinned the chieftain's thighs, and covered his cartouch-box with it. I was astonished to see with what boldness and precision Aranghie drew his designs on the skin and what beautiful ornaments he produced. No rule and compasses could be more exact than the lines and circles he formed.

Budding artists acquired their craft by working on those who were unable to afford the charge of the professional artist. If the professional suspected that remuneration would be ungenerous, his work became careless. On the other hand, as Robley puts it: 'Presents and payments flowed into the coffers of the man of talent from all quarters, according to the means and ability of the givers. Double-barrelled guns, canoes, clothes, and even slaves have been presented to these distinguished persons as marks of the esteem in which their talents were held'.

## A Trade in Tattoed Heads

It was not uncommon in New Zealand for the Maoris to preserve heads after death by embalming them—a practice maintained not only by the family in an attempt to keep alive the memory of the dead, but also by the conqueror in time of war. This was no new idea, as it had been practised long before by the Scythians, the Gauls, the Early Britons and the American Indians. . . .

The first dried head to be acquired by Europeans was bought by Sir Joseph Banks on 20 January 1770. The natives apparently exhibited the greatest reluctance to the sale of the head and could not be induced to part with another at that time.

This resistance disappeared all too soon. The traders found that there was a demand at home for tattooed heads, and museums and private collectors were prepared to pay generously for good specimens. The Maoris willingly exchanged old preserved heads for firearms with which to wage their tribal wars. Heads became scarce. With the realization that their chances of victory were enormously increased with the new weapons, the pace of the slaughter was stepped up in order to acquire new heads with which to barter anew. Very often the heads belonged to untattooed slaves, but this small defect was simple to rectify post mortem, for a newly tattooed head looked just as well when preserved as the antique specimen. . . .

## A Grotesque Enterprise

The sordid tale degenerates yet further. A trader, interviewing a Maori chief on board his ship, showed disapproval at the standard of Moko on the dried heads being offered for sale and pointed out that it did no justice to the skill of the native artists. The chief, realizing the force of the argument, turned round to his entourage with the remark, 'Choose which of these heads you like best, and when you come back I will take care to have it dried and ready for your acceptance'.

Other dealers, looking for good heads on living slaves, were not unseldom 'overtaken by a fate which deserves little pity'. [One of General Robley's officers] Maning accidentally came across what he thought to be a company of natives, but which were in fact a collection of heads stuck on rods, with cross pieces at shoulder level, covered with cloaks so as to appear very lifelike. . . .

By 1831 the traffic had reached such horrific proportions that Governor Darling issued a proclamation drawing attention to a state of affairs which had to stop. Shortly afterwards an Act was passed which made such dealings illegal, and the possession of a dried head a punishable offence, even, theoretically, in the case of a museum.

## A Lost Art

Once a tattooed head had lost its commercial value, and with the arrival of the missionaries, Moko started to decline. It was soon appreciated that any person coming to live at a mission station should no longer submit himself to the operation. When King Tawhiao died in 1894 at the age of seventy the last really fine specimen of Moko was lost to the world. Ten years previously, on his futile visit to England to see Queen Victoria, . . . Brock and Co. included in their Display at the Crystal Palace a special pyrotechnical representation of his face. As Robley commented, 'It was reserved for that celebrated firm of fireworkers to achieve the apotheosis of Moko'.

# 2

# The Basics of Tattoos and Body Piercings

# Considerations for Getting a Tattoo

SoYouWanna.com

In order to avoid the grief of a poorly executed (and permanent) tattoo, an individual needs to give thoughtful consideration to the procedure, the artist, and the design. Although reputation is important, the tattooist should be someone the patron feels comfortable with. The client should also consider the parlor itself; an unsanitary or unkempt place of business may increase the risk of disease or infection. The choice of design will usually hinge on both aesthetic preferences and financial factors. The following viewpoint from SoYouWanna.com summarizes the basic points a person should consider before sitting down in the chair to get a tattoo.

YOU'VE FINALLY DECIDED TO JOIN THE COUNTER-culture and get yourself a wicked-looking tat, but you don't know where to go? Or perhaps you've already got a tattoo or two, but you can't figure out why it looks faded and blotchy and you're saying to yourself "But that fat guy at the biker convention seemed so competent and reliable!" Either way, we're sure there are things you'd like to know before you get large quantities of ink permanently injected into your flesh. What follows is intended for the thoughtful tattoo-seeker; if your plan involves a drunken stupor and a rusty razor, we think you'll find this article a little too conscious about safety. However, if you think about things before you do them, even when you're trying to look like a bad-ass, this will give you much food for thought.

And yes, it hurts. But not *that* much.

■

# Safety and Hygiene Considerations

The first thing you've got to think about when you consider getting a tattoo is that it involves someone sticking needles into you. Now who do you trust to have enough respect for hygiene to stick needles in you? Your doctor, probably, but who else? Some greasy, leering guy in a tent at an outdoor concert? Your friend's buddy, who works out of his basement? No and no. You trust people who act very much like doctors, when it comes to hygiene, and no one else.

Sure, a lot of tattoo studios look pretty Goth, with black and purple paint and vampiric-looking staff, but if it's clean black and purple paint you shouldn't let that part worry you. However, if you get the impression that there's anything dingy or unkempt about the place, you should take that as insufficient concern about cleanliness and find somewhere else to go. Choosing a tattoo artist is a serious decision, for a lot of reasons . . . and you should feel comfortable asking your tattoo artist about safety, cleanliness, his or her experience, and anything else which is important to you. If you don't feel comfortable talking to your prospective artist, look elsewhere. Be picky. The basic idea is that you want to find a place that is as clean as your doctor's office, even though it might not have posters of amiable-looking goats or other farm animals on the walls and mobiles hanging from the ceilings.

Specific things for which you must watch are:

1. Most importantly, a brand new sterile needle must be used every time.
2. All other tools that are involved in the tattooing process must be either sterilized or disposable (and, of course, they must be either sterilized or disposed of after each customer).
3. Everything should be personally laid-out for your tattoo. You don't want to share in a big communal bottle of ink with your fellow tattoo-lovers; you want little individual disposable containers of ink just for you. Latex gloves. Vaseline should be dispensed with disposable instruments—not by hand. You get the idea.
4. Non-disposable equipment should be sterilized with an autoclave (an apparatus which uses superheated steam under high pressure to sterilize instruments), not an

ultra-sonic cleaner or a dunk in a tub of rubbing alcohol. Ask the tattoo artist if his/her autoclave is FDA-regulated. Wiping with a greasy rag, Windex, and spit-shining are also, while quaint, unacceptable.

Don't allow the foregoing advice to leave you with a bad impression of tattoo artists in general. There are many, many tattoo artists who maintain spotlessly clean and scrupulously hygienic studios. We just want to ensure that you realize how important it is to find one of them. Of course, a commitment to cleanliness is not all you want. The following section tells you how to find a tattoo artist who will ink you with the kind of artistry you deserve. Let's just assume you deserve something really fabulous.

## Choosing a Tattoo Artist

There are three main concerns when choosing a tattoo artist:
1. Is he or she any good?
2. Do you feel comfortable talking to him or her?
3. Can you afford it?

## Is He or She Any Good?

The only way to tell whether or not an artist is good is to see examples of his or her work. Recommendations are helpful, of course, but the recommendations should carry infinitely more weight if the recommender is proffering a tattooed example of the artist's work. There are plenty of awesome artists out there who, though you wouldn't deny their skills, just don't appeal to you with the style of tats they do. So don't take anyone else's word for it—get a look at the artist's work yourself. Furthermore, and don't start thinking we're paranoid, but it's best to see actual examples of the work on a live person who can tell you who did the work. Anyone can put up a bunch of pictures and claim authorship.

You can meet people and talk to them about their tattoos at tattoo conventions, in the tattoo studios you visit and on the street or at a club, so long as you're not an idiot about it. People are usually proud of their tattoos, and if you seem genuinely interested a lot of people will be happy to tell you about their ink. Tattoo magazines are also a good source for information. The photo-essays they publish about various artists are likely to be well-researched and legitimate examples of the artists' work. There are also websites, such as TattooStudios.com, which show examples of artists' work. The key is to shop around and find someone really capable, because the quality of your tattoo depends so much on the talent of the tattoo artist.

## Do You Feel Comfortable Talking to Him or Her?

This is important for safety reasons, of course, but it's also important because you have to communicate what you want in a tattoo. If you don't feel comfortable talking to your tattoo artist, it's not likely that you'll get what you want. You don't have to be best buddies with the artist, but you need to be able to talk to him or her without reserve and with some certainty that your desires will be met.

## Can You Afford It?

As you shop around for a good tattoo artist, you are likely to find several whose work really appeals to you. Whether you can afford them is another matter, but something you must take into account. They will not necessarily live in the same city as you, and even if they do, they might charge a lot of money for their work. Before you get too far into it, you should figure out if it's really feasible for you to work with a certain artist. You might want to call an artist to get a general idea of what your tattoo would cost—some artists will give you a rough idea over the phone, but some won't. If the artist lives far away, you're likely to have to pay for plane fare, a hotel and the cost of the tattoo. Don't bother getting all worked up about being tattooed by a certain person, and don't waste either of your time, if you can't afford to pay all the necessary costs.

The cost of getting a tattoo varies from artist to artist. Popular artists can charge more, while incompetent or inexperienced artists will be cheaper. Artists will usually charge a flat rate for their flash designs, and this will depend on the size and color of the design. You can expect to pay approximately $50 to $100 for a "flash" [a stock design] of about two square inches. For custom work, artists will usually charge by the hour, but they might negotiate prices with you ahead of time based on how difficult the design is and how long they think it

## Tattoo Myths

*A tattoo will change your life.* Only if your self image is as shallow as your skin. Don't lay some heavy mystical-type expectation on your decision to get tattooed. On the other hand, the decision is permanent. Choose the design, location, and art wisely.

*Any good artist can do any tattoo.* Not necessarily. While most professionals are capable of a variety of styles, they usually have a specialty, a unique style of tattooing they've developed and are very good at. That artist who's known for his killer tribal work may not be the choice for the portrait of mom and dad you've been planning. Match the design you want with the artist who can pull it off.

*Wall certificates prove that it's a good tattoo shop.* Not necessarily. With the exception of "APT" certificates, which show the artist is affiliated with a professional organization concerned with safe, sterile tattooing procedures, most other "certificates" claiming professional status are merely wallpaper freebies from supply companies.

"Tattoo Myths, Legends, and Lies," www.imagesinink.net.

will take. The hourly rate for custom work ranges from $50 to $300. Don't go for bargains. A cheap tattoo will look cheap. You should try to find an artist who charges between $100 and $150 per hour. If money is no object and you simply must have a popular, expensive artist work on you, then go ahead and spend more.

## Choosing a Design

The classic mistake is, of course, tattooing yourself with the name of your main squeeze. You go ahead and do it if you feel you must, but imagine finding yourself in a quandary about whether to stay in a relationship and finding that one of the considerations is that you must keep your skin art contemporary. Beside that, there are so many other interesting meaningful designs which you can choose that can't take off with all your NoMeansNo albums.

The most important thing to consider is the permanence of tattoos. You have to choose something which will always be meaningful to you, and that's hard to know. How many things did you think were really cool five years ago which make you cringe now? You have to think carefully about what sort of image or design has the kind of lasting significance to you that you cannot imagine being erased by time. The tattoo ain't going anywhere unless you put in more money and a few more hours in the chair, and even then it's not going to look perfect.

## Styles of Tattoos

The basic distinction in tattoos is between "flash" or stock tattoos and custom tattoos. Flash tattoos are the ones pictured on the walls which range from standard old favorites like anchors, hearts, skulls, and dragons to the artist's custom designs that he or she is willing to do for a flat rate. Custom tattoos are designed or requested by you, and then worked out with the tattoo artist. You can draw your tattoo yourself, get a friend to draw it, or tell the artist what you want and get him or her to draw it. The artist will have to do some work with it anyway, to create an outline, and when he or she is finished adapting your drawing or idea you should check and make sure it is what you wanted. . . .

## Caring for Your New Tattoo

Your new tattoo is an open wound. Let's make sure it doesn't turn into a *festering* open wound. Leave the bandage on for at least twelve hours, and when you take it off, be nice. If it won't come off right away, use warm water to help it off. Let it dry for about an hour, then wash the crud off (don't ask us to go into detail, but it'll be there) with a gentle soap. Then apply a thin coat of Polysporin or another antibiotic cream. For the next four or five days you'll want to wash it gently and reapply the cream twice per day. Do so in the shower, not the bath, as the new tattoo should not be submerged in water for any great length of time. That means no swimming, no hot tubs, no baths and no sex in the shower for about two weeks after you get tattooed. After four or five days you should switch to a water-based cream such as Moisturel until your tattoo is completely healed. As with any open wound, you must not allow it to get dirty and you should keep your damn hands off it. No picking, scratching, or other dorking around until it's healed. It will scab over a bit while it's healing, but that's natural and you should not feel compelled to try to remove the scab.

For those of you who are too hardcore to worry about your health, this is not just about health. You can think of it as primarily about making sure your tattoo looks its best, because if you mess with it while it's healing, the colors can run together, it can fade and if it gets infected the resulting wound could cause enough scar tissue to mar your work of art seriously.

# The Tattoo Procedure

Karen Hudson

The tattoo process involves much more than simply deciding on a design and getting stuck with needles. A myriad of paperwork must be completed before the client even sits down in the chair. Then the skin is shaved, the implements are disinfected, and a stencil is drawn—all before a needle ever meets the patron's skin.

Tattoo enthusiast Karen Hudson has learned much about the complex process of tattooing during her tutelage under a master tattoo artist. In the following article for About.com, Hudson guides the reader through the steps she has become so familiar with.

IF YOU ARE THINKING ABOUT GETTING YOUR first tattoo, but are unfamiliar with the process, the thought might meet you with anticipation. Fear of the unknown can sometimes hold us back from doing things we really want to do. You might be concerned that it will hurt too much. You might be worried that you wouldn't know if the artist was doing something wrong.

The best thing you can do is educate yourself on the process of the tattoo application, and that way you will be prepared and know what to expect when you sit in the artist's chair. So, how is a tattoo applied to the skin? From start to finish, this article will tell you exactly how the human skin is transformed into a beautiful work of art. *Please keep in mind that the following outline describes the most favorable situation for getting a tattoo. There will always be differences between one artist*

■

*and the next, but any major deviance from these guidelines could in-dicate a problem.*

# Paperwork, Payment, and Preparation

Once you have decided on your tattoo design and your artist, you will be required to show valid identification for proof of age. You may also be asked for your address and phone number, so your artist can contact you in the future if need be. In most studios, payment must be made before services are ren-dered. It is up to each studio to decide which methods of pay-ment they accept. Whatever method you pay with, make sure they give you a receipt.

After your paperwork is filled out, you will be seated in the tattoo chair. Sometimes this is in an open work area, and some-times a private room depending on the location of your tattoo. If you are shy and don't want others to watch, you can request a private room, but be sure you have done this in advance. A lot of studios use dentist-style chairs, some use regular table chairs, and some use benches. Your artist will do his or her best to make you comfortable for the tattoo you have chosen.

Now it is time for the preparation. The area of your body you have chosen for your tattoo will be cleaned, usually with rubbing alcohol. Then, any hair will be removed from the area by shaving it with a new disposable razor, which will be dis-carded after being used. [The area] will be cleaned again to make sure it is smooth and ready for the transfer.

# Applying the Stencil and Preparing the Tattoo Machine

Most studios today use a wonderful machine called a thermal-fax to make their stencils. This saves on literally hours of trac-ing time by simply inserting your tattoo design into the ma-chine and [transferring] it onto a special thermal paper in seconds. Once your stencil is ready, it's time to create the transfer onto your skin. Some artists will use soap or water to moisten the skin, and some will use stick deodorant. These aid in making the design transfer better and darker onto your skin. When the paper is pulled away from your skin, it will leave you with a purple-ish blue likeness of your future tattoo!

It is at this time that your artist will start preparing the tattoo machine. The inks will be placed in little tiny cups called "ink caps," and the needles and tubes will be removed from their sterile pouches and placed in the machine. Clean, distilled water will be poured into a cup for cleaning the needles during the tattoo process and to change from one color to the next. Some . . . ointment or Vaseline will be placed on a clean surface for your use only.

## Drawing the Tattoo

Now it is time to get down to serious business! A little ointment will be placed over your transfer design for a few reasons. One is that it helps keep the transfer on longer without accidentally rubbing it off, and it also helps the needle to slide along the skin more smoothly, which is certainly going to be more comfortable to you! After the ointment is applied, it is time for the first line. If you're nervous, don't hold your breath. Some people have passed out during a tattoo, and trust me—it wasn't the pain, it was the panic! Take a nice, slow, deep breath and try to relax. The first minute or so will be the roughest. After that, your skin will kind of get used to it and the pain will subside.

Once all the linework is done, your artist can breathe a little bit easier knowing that they won't have to worry about the transfer anymore. Now it's time to get creative with a little shading and possibly color. Depending on the size of your tattoo, your artist may switch to a different set of needles called "magnums" which are designed for coloring and shading. They may even switch tattoo machines altogether. The shading and coloring can go along quite quickly, and before you know it . . . you've got a complete tattoo.

## Documentation and Aftercare

Your artist may like a picture of your tattoo for their portfolio. They'll clean it up real good, and sometimes even apply a hot towel to it first. Then they'll take a picture, and this is a good time for you to get a shot, too, if you brought a camera along. Taking a photo after the protective ointment is applied causes a glare, so it is best to do it now. If for any reason you do not want the artist to take a photo, just say so. You are not under obligation to let them.

Now that your tattoo is finished and clean, it needs to be treated just like a wound. A protective layer of ointment will be applied to the tattoo to prevent invasion of airborne bacteria that can cause infection. Then a bandage will be applied, and it will be taped up to make sure it is secure. It is important that you keep this bandage on for the amount of time your artist instructs, which brings us to our last step: aftercare.

Your artist will now give you aftercare instructions. These should be given both verbally and on a piece of paper for you to take home with you. It is important that you listen and follow the instructions you are given. From this point on, it is your responsibility to make sure your tattoo is well taken care of. The artist cannot be blamed if you get an infection because you didn't follow directions.

## A Happy Customer, A Happy Artist

You are now the proud owner of a beautiful tattoo. Before you walk out the door, thank your artist, and please don't forget to tip them. Show how much you appreciate their work and dedication. Refer your friends to them. When you go back for your next tattoo, you will have established a good relationship with your artist, and you can be assured they will be there to help you if you ever have any problems or questions in the future.

# The Perils of Piercing

Jane E. Brody

In their zeal to follow the latest body modification fads, teenagers are moving beyond the pierced ear to more unusual parts of their bodies—noses, navels, eyebrows, tongues, lips, and even genitals. In the following article for the *New York Times*, Associated Press writer Jane E. Brody points out that many youths do not adequately consider the potential consequences of these more extreme modifications. Body piercings sometimes result in complications such as allergies, infections, scars, and slow healing, and persons with visible piercings may be shunned or even discriminated against at school or work.

FANS OF PIERCING HAVE BEEN CREATIVE IN FINDing unusual body parts to adorn. The fads of teenagers can run from the ridiculous to the absurd: leaving shoelaces untied, sucking on pacifiers, dyeing hair five different colors, wearing pants so big they expose half the buttocks. Parents may cringe at such weird behavior, but most adults realize that battles over teenagers' styles are futile, the fads will soon fade and the damage won't be permanent. But the situation can be quite different when it comes to this craze: body piercing. People, many of them fad-driven teenagers, boast of holes in their ears, noses, navels, nipples, eyebrows, lips, tongues, cheeks and in some cases even their genitals. And some are putting their health on the line when they pierce themselves or one another or rely on unlicensed operators who know little about aseptic technique or the medical risks incurred when holes are stabbed through various body parts. Even those who head to the mall to have their ears or noses pierced by jewelry sales clerks may be asking for trouble.

Many who call themselves "piercing professionals" have had no formal training and may have learned the techniques from seminars, videos or magazines, or as apprentices to other so-called professionals. All too often, the decision to get pierced through, say, the tongue or the nipple is made with little consideration of the pain involved, the potential hazards and the long recovery time. Fifteen-year-old David, for example, had his tongue pierced against his father's wishes. For more than a week, he could hardly talk and could eat little other than mush. Even when the swelling receded, his tongue still hurt, his speech was affected, and his father refused to talk to him. David's warning: "Not only make sure you have a long, hard think about a tongue-pierce, but think of the consequences and things that might happen afterward. When one says that the first five or six days is close to hell, you won't fully understand it until you get a tongue-pierce." Some fad-driven teenagers are learning that a stud in the tongue can have its drawbacks. Another teenager who had some regrets cautioned his peers "to consider their career choices or college choices because of others' reactions" to certain piercings.

## Body Piercing Complications

In a recent issue of *Emergency Medicine,* a medical magazine, Dr. Charles Stewart of Colorado Springs and the Dakota Heartland Hospital in Fargo summarized the various complications that have been known to result from body piercing.

*ALLERGY*—Most common are allergic reactions to the jewelry inserted, especially if it is brass-plated or contains nickel. The allergy typically results in a weeping, crusting, itchy wound. To avoid this problem, "body jewelry should be made of surgical-grade stainless steel, 14-karat yellow or white gold, or titanium," Dr. Stewart wrote.

*INFECTION*—Almost as common and potentially far more serious are infections, which result in redness, swelling, tenderness and pain and often swelling of nearby glands. When sterile techniques are not used, bacteria and viruses can be introduced into the bloodstream, including the hepatitis B virus that can cause chronic hepatitis and liver cancer, and HIV, the virus that causes AIDS. In people born with heart valve disorders, bacterial endocarditis, a potentially deadly infection of the heart, can result if they fail to take preventive antibiotics. A Mayo Clinic study of 445 patients with congenital heart disease revealed that nearly one in four developed endocarditis after body piercing. Piercing the nose can result in a staphylo-

*Many people get pierced without taking into consideration infection or the possibility of permanent scarring.*

coccal infection and piercing the cartilaginous part of the ear, which has a very poor blood supply, can result in a pseudo-monas infection, necessitating surgery and resulting in permanent deformity. Even tetanus is a risk in people who have not been immunized in the last 10 years.

*UNSIGHTLY SCARS AND INJURY*—Some people, most commonly African-Americans and people from Mediterranean areas, develop large, ugly scars that may have to be surgically removed. Also, if piercing jewelry catches on something, the tissue can be ripped. Piercing of the tongue can result in permanent numbness, difficulty talking, loss of taste and breathing problems if swelling is severe. The jewelry inserted in a pierced tongue can cause teeth to fracture or the lining of the mouth to become chronically inflamed.

*MOVEMENT OR REJECTION*—The jewelry may move or the hole become thin and narrow, causing scarring, inflammation and prolonged healing. Mechanical stress is a common cause, for example, when the jewelry is under pressure or friction from clothing, or the piercing has been placed in an area that changes shape with body movement, or the jewelry used is too thin or too thick and heavy for the tissue in which it is inserted.

## Considering the Consequences

Start by asking friends who have been pierced about their experiences and what they would suggest if they were to do it all over again. Think about your future. How will adults who interview you for school admission or jobs react when they see your piercings? One young woman was fired from a law firm because the rest of the staff was so repulsed by her multiple facial piercings. Become as well informed as possible about the procedure, its risks and how long it is likely to take for the piercing to heal. Are you willing to tolerate whatever pain and complications that might ensue, regardless of how long they last? And are you willing to adhere to postpiercing cleaning techniques for as long as they are needed? Kelly A. Muldoon, a pediatric nurse practitioner in Bridgeport, Conn., pointed out in the *Journal of Pediatric Health Care* that "healing times vary from about eight weeks to more than a year, depending on the site pierced." Throughout this time, one must adhere to strict hygienic practices and avoid touching the hole or the jewelry except to clean them.

Piercing should be done only by a well-trained professional who practices sterile techniques, wearing new disposable gloves and using disposable tools (make sure a new package is opened in front of you and look for brown sterile markings on the package). Nondisposable tools must be sterilized between uses in a steam autoclave. A piercing gun is safe only for piercing the ear lobe, not the cartilaginous part of the ear or any other body part, which should be pierced only with a proper gauge needle. Ms. Muldoon cautioned that jewelry used in ear piercings should not be used in any other area of the body.

Some states require parental permission to pierce a minor. If your parents say no, forget about it. Don't use a piercer willing to skirt the law, and never pierce yourself or a friend. Dr. Stewart said many operators were "hucksters who, after attending a single piercing seminar, set up a 'studio' with the hope of making a fast buck." Don't rely on the Internet for information about piercing or access to piercers. Dr. Stewart pointed out that much of the information on Web sites is "biased, erroneous or downright misleading."

# Henna Tattoos:
# The Art of Mehndi

Rupal C. Pinto

For those who are concerned about the finality of a permanent tattoo, there is a temporary alternative. The henna tattoo, which derives from the ancient art of mehndi, can be applied and worn for a few weeks with no long-term effects. Henna tattoos have been donned by modern popular icons such as Madonna and Prince, and the art has become a rising trend in mainstream culture. In the following viewpoint, henna artist Rupal C. Pinto traces the traditional roots of mehndi, explains the preparation, application, and removal of the dye, and discusses possible drawbacks of the body art form.

MEHNDI IS THE TRADITIONAL ART OF HENNA painting in India and the Middle East. You may see it written as mehandi, mehendi, mendhi, henna, al-henna, and a myriad other names and spellings. In recent times, United States henna artists have come to denote the art with the term "Henna Body Art." All of these words describe the same timeless art form, body painting for festive occasions. However you spell it, mehndi is pronounced meh-hen-di (with a soft, dental d sound like "thee").

## The Mehndi Tradition

I specialize in understanding conceptions of henna in India, where it has been used since the 12th century. Many historical documents outline earlier use; for example, it is the Arabic Muslims who brought henna to India, where it has blossomed

■

into its own unique art style. In Indian mehndi, a person applies designs traditionally to a woman's hands and feet. For particularly auspicious occasions, men apply mehndi as well. The most auspicious occasion warranting mehndi artwork is the Indian wedding, where both bride and bridegroom apply henna, as well as several members of the bridal party. Henna on any occasion symbolizes fertility. At the wedding, henna artwork additionally symbolizes the love between husband and wife, and the stain's long-lasting nature symbolizes the enduring nature of their love.

Mehndi came into use because of its cooling therapeutic effect in a hot climate, and, in India, it was also a way for a bride and groom to get to know one another before an arranged marriage. A variety of traditions underlie the use of mehndi, including wedding games and legends. For example, the groom's name is usually written somewhere within the bride's mehndi; if he cannot find his name within the intricate design, the bride is said to have the control in the marriage. Also, a dark mehndi design for both bride and groom signifies that the two will have a strong relationship. Within the past few years, mehndi has become popularized in the West by musicians and Hollywood personalities alike, and is now a quickly rising trend among women and men in world culture.

## Preparing and Applying Henna Dye

Translating the word "henna" literally means "to become queen." The Indian name "mehndi" designates the process, the dye, and the stain of mehndi. To make the dye, henna (mehndi) leaves are dried and finely ground. The powder that results is filtered two or more times through a fine nylon cloth. This process results in removing the coarse fibers from the powder, making what is left finer and easier to use. The artist then mixes this fine powder with an oil (such as eucalyptus, nilgiri, or mehndi oil) and other liquids (lemon, water, or tea), making a thick paste. This paste is applied to the wearer's hand in various designs, which can range from large, thick patterns to Moroccan geometric patterns to traditional Indian paisleys and lace-like drawings. All depends upon the skill of the artist and the style of designs used. A solution of lemon juice and sugar is then applied to the drying mehndi to allow it to remain stuck to the skin and to improve the dying process.

After 2–12 hours, during which the mehndi dries, the wearer scrapes the paste off to reveal the designs, which resemble tattoos and last 1–3 weeks on the skin. While the color of the mehndi dye is a deep shade of green, once removed the dye leaves a color varying from light orange to a deep brownish-black. . . .

Mehndi usually lasts for at least one to two weeks. I have heard of people saying that mehndi can last from two to four weeks; however, this figure is misleading because the length mehndi will stay depends on a number of factors.

> How often you wash your hands
> What kind of soap you use
> Your skin quality and heat in your body
> Location of the mehndi on the body
> The ingredients you add to your henna paste

Henna works by staining the outer layers of the epidermis, permanently. The reason why your stain itself is impermanent is because of a magical, mystical, mystery. Or not. Your skin exfoliates off, right? So the deeper your mehndi stains, the longer your design lasts. Thus, it is important to be aware of the contributing factors to a henna design's latency. Strong soap and hand-washing shortens the life of a henna stain because it exfoliates your skin. Therefore, after getting mehndi applied, do not wash your skin for at least twelve hours, and do not use any harsh antibacterial soaps as long as the stain remains upon your skin. If we take our exfoliation theory farther, we note the palm of one's hands exfoliates much faster than the back of the hands; thus, henna on the palm lasts less than half as long as henna on the back of the hand.

Adding essential oils adds another dimension to henna; while the oils, which contain terpenes, can increase the stain quality of the henna, they will greatly compromise the staining depth of your henna, and thus will make the stain disappear in one week rather than the normal 1–3 weeks.

# How to Remove Henna

Given the qualities of a henna design, you can use my tips in a converse manner. When you and your friends first start doing mehndi artwork, you may end up with a disastrous mehndi design. But do not lose hope. If you decide that your design is not up to par, follow these instructions.

1. *Remove the henna paste immediately:* I know this goes without saying, and you probably noticed that you didn't like the design only after you removed the henna, but removing the henna quickly after application, using water, will prevent the henna dye from sinking below the most external layers of skin.

2. *Take a bath:* Seriously now, a nice soak in hot water will not only keep you cool, calm and collected, but it will also cause your skin to exfoliate; thus, the layers of skin which have absorbed the henna design will flake off sooner if you soak it in water. Many artists suggest that you soak in a hot tub—the chlorine in the tub will definitely help to take the henna right off.

3. *Wash your hands:* Stronger soaps, like a soak in the hot tub, cause skin to exfoliate to a greater degree. To get rid of henna sooner, choose the antibacterial soap at your local drug store instead of regular glycerin.

4. *Wait:* I have to tell you that there is no hard and fast way to remove henna from the skin immediately. Some artists recommend soaks in mild, diluted bleaches. In general, use my tips carefully; scrubbing too hard and soaking in the bath for too long may just give you red, prune-shaped fingertips.

Chances are, however, that you will love your mehndi design and will want to keep it on your skin for as long as possible. But remember that mehndi is no ordinary tattoo, and as time passes, your henna will fade. Body heat and skin quality have a great deal to do with the quality of the design on a particular person. People who have drier skin and a lot of body heat tend to have darker mehndi. I have known people who have had a mehndi design on for over a month for this reason alone. And I think that some people just always get good henna stains. I'll call these lucky ones *"hennaphilic."*

# Hennaing Dark Skin

Avoid the misconception that being darker skinned prevents you from being able to have dark mehndi. This is certainly not the case. Although people with very dark skin may have to use only the best henna pastes, skin color has very little to do with the final hue of the dye. As a dark-skinned Indian myself, I can tell you that my mehndi comes out as a dark brown on both sides of my hands, and I can get a nice, dark sienna on my legs. If you are African-American, for example, don't be afraid to try mehndi. If your skin is very dark and you believe you would not be able to receive the correct contrast between your skin and the henna, try your design first on the palms of your hands; this area of the skin inevitably takes henna better than other parts of the skin in people of every color. Perhaps start with a small design to be sure, but be assured that even some very fair-skinned people can't get a good stain out of the mehndi. And remember that this is an art that is used all over the world, on people of all different skin colors.

## Strategies for a Long-Lasting Design

All too often I receive e-mails from people who wonder why they got a nicely colored henna design while their friend's design did not get beyond a light orange (the message comes of the other way around as well). Plainly and simply, people are different from one another and different skin types take dyes differently. When you compare your design with a friend's don't just consider ethnicity differences, consider the skin quality differences which go with the ethnicity. At the same time, feel free to experiment; your skin might need more or less essential oils to get a good design. Work at it, get the best henna powder, do your work till you get the chemistry right.

So, to optimize the quality of your mehndi design, choose a place on your skin that is free from oils. Make sure it is clean, dry, and hairless. Do not add lotion to the skin before putting henna on it; your henna will slide right off, or it will at least result in a coloring less vibrant than you would otherwise be able to attain. Furthermore, certain parts of the body work better than others due to variations in oiliness of skin and body temperature. Usually the palms of the hand and soles of the feet work optimally for mehndi design. I also like to apply mehndi to the back of the hand, wrists, lower arm, tops of feet and sometimes the shins. The best skin prep for a henna design is a light swipe with an alcohol swab or witch hazel; if you don't have these, just wash your skin well with soap and water.

Please note that you will have less luck with an armband or navel mehndi design than you will have with an anklet or bracelet. If you choose to put the mehndi on a cool body part (versus the hands), the time that it lasts can vary. For example, the inner side of a mehndi armband tends to be darker-stained than the outside of your arm. That is not to say that the mehndi stain will definitely be bad if you get it done as an armband or such; you just have to make sure that you leave the mehndi on as long as possible to get the most out of your design. Also, if you choose to apply mehndi, you always stand the risk that the color will not come out as dark as you want it to. The darkness of the mehndi depends strongly on skin type and where you apply the mehndi. Mehndi will always come out better on the palm of your hand than on the back; however, on the palm of the hand, the mehndi washes off more quickly.

## The Drawbacks of Mehndi

Whether or not to get mehndi is also an important decision because of other properties of henna. For example, henna leaves have a very distinctive scent, and after the mehndi dye is removed from a person, his/her skin will still retain this scent. Many people like the scent, which usually resembles a combination of eucalyptus and henna and various other essential oils, but it is very strong and can become bothersome and distracting. Additionally, other enhancing products, such as tea, coffee, cloves, lemon, and lime, are sometimes added to mehndi—and all of these ingredients can increase the scent. The good and bad thing about the scent of henna is that the oil scents usually wear off after a few days; the henna scent stays for the first 4–5 days. A way to alleviate the scent problem is to place the mehndi on a part which you don't hold near your face too often, such as the foot. People who are sensitive to perfumes should definitely think twice before getting mehndi done, although the scent probably won't remain with you for the *entire* two weeks of the stain's duration (most often the scent lasts for a few days into having the stain). I for one, love the stain of henna, and sit around smelling my fingertips whenever I have a design, but not everyone feels the same way I do!

Before choosing to get mehndi applied on yourself, you

should also carefully consider whether it's the right time. Henna designs are expensive, and you probably should be willing to keep the paste on your hands for an extended period of time—at least 2 hours—if you wish to get a dark, long-lasting stain. Plus, will henna get you in trouble with work? As for me, I wear henna wherever I go, but as a hennafanatic be prepared to get comments—great ones at first, but more questioning ones later on. As the mehndi starts to fade it may look blotchy.

# Links Between Tattooing and Hepatitis C

Peggy Peck

Hepatitis C, a silent but sometimes deadly virus, infects an estimated four million Americans. Former Centers for Disease Control researcher Robert Haley, MD, believes that tattooing is a major, but often-overlooked, cause of Hepatitis C infection. Ironically, Haley points out, the risk of infection is greater at commercial tattoo parlors than with either do-it-yourself tattoos or prison tattoos. In the following excerpt, award-winning medical writer Peggy Peck, a regular contributor to *WebMD Medical News*, considers the links between tattooing and Hepatitis C.

BETH BLACKMARR, 38, IS AN INSURANCE EXECUtive in Cleveland, Ohio. In a business suit, briefcase in hand, she is all button-down, no-nonsense professional. But under the suit she carries five permanent reminders of her life as a teenager in LaGrange, Kentucky—five tattoos.

Blackmarr tells WebMD that she got the tattoos at a commercial tattoo parlor when she was in her teens. She says she now wishes she could get the tattoos removed, but "I've never been overly concerned about health problems because of the tattoos." That, however, may change.

## Tattoos and Hepatitis C

A new study by a former Centers for Disease Control researcher suggests that getting a tattoo can significantly increase the risk

■

of hepatitis C, a viral infection of the liver for which there is no cure and which often leads to fatal liver disease.

Hepatitis C is considered a major public health risk because it is a silent disease, which lies dormant for decades before it flares up. The CDC estimates that 4 million Americans are infected with hepatitis C and about 10,000 people die from the disease each year.

Although there is no cure, the disease is treated with a combination of an antiviral drug called ribavarin and immune therapy with interferon. The treatment is very long—48 weeks—and is difficult to tolerate because of unpleasant side effects including headaches, constant nausea, fatigue, and depression.

Hepatitis C is spread by blood-to-blood contamination, says lead study author Robert Haley, MD, chief of epidemiology at the University of Texas Southwestern Medical Center (UTSW) in Dallas. Injection drug abusers have an increased risk for hepatitis C because they often share needles. Health-care workers, especially nurses, are also considered high risk for hepatitis C because of "accidental needle sticks," he says. And because the nation's blood supply was not tested for hepatitis C until about 10 years ago, blood transfusions before 1991 are also considered a risk factor for transmission of hepatitis C.

## The Missing Risk Factor

"But when all the known risk factors are considered, the majority of hepatitis C cases are still not accounted for," says Haley, who worked for more than 10 years at the CDC before joining the faculty at UTSW. "That's because tattoos were left out of the equation. When we consider tattoos as a risk factor we can explain the difference."

"People who had do-it-yourself tattoos have a three times greater risk for hepatitis C than people without tattoos, and people tattooed in jail have an even higher risk. But the greatest risk comes from commercial tattoo parlors," he says. "People who get tattoos at commercial tattoo parlors have a nine times greater risk."

He bases his risk calculations on a study of over 600 people who were patients at a spine clinic in the early 1990s. The patients agreed to be evaluated for blood-borne infections, says Haley. The evaluation included detailed information about lifestyle risk factors as well as blood tests.

Haley found that 113 patients had at least one tattoo and 22% of those patients tested positive for hepatitis C. "Only 3.5% of the patients with no tattoos had hepatitis C," he says.

## Differing Risk Interpretations

The news about tattoos is welcomed but not surprising, says Thelma King Thiel, who runs the Hepatitis Foundation International, an educational-advocacy group based in Cedar Grove, New Jersey. Thiel's group sponsors Hepatitis Awareness Month in May.

# The Centers for Disease Control's Position on Tattooing and Hepatitis C

Although some studies have found an association between tattooing and HCV [Hepatitis C] infection in very selected populations, it is not known if these results can be generalized to the whole population. Any percutaneous exposure has the potential for transferring infectious blood and potentially transmitting bloodborne pathogens; however, no data exist in the United States indicating that persons with exposures to tattooing alone are at increased risk for HCV infection. For example, during the past 20 years, less than 1% of persons with newly acquired hepatitis C reported to CDC's sentinel surveillance system gave a history of being tattooed. Further studies are needed to determine if these types of exposures, and the settings in which they occur, are risk factors for HCV infection in the United States. CDC is currently conducting a large study to evaluate tattooing as a potential risk.

"CDC's Position on Tattooing and HCV Infection," Centers for Disease Control, www.cdc.gov.

"We say that anything that invades the body by piercing the skin is a risk factor," says Thiel. She says that as soon as she saw Haley's paper "I shot a copy right off to the CDC." Thiel and Haley would like the CDC to officially designate tattooing as a risk factor for hepatitis C.

The CDC, which does list tattooing as a risk factor for hepatitis B, has stopped short of linking tattoos to hepatitis C. It states simply that more research is needed.

Brooke Seckel, MD, director of cosmetic surgery at Boston's Lahey Clinic and an assistant professor of surgery at Harvard Medical School, is an ardent opponent of tattoos. Seckel says the medical community was recently dealt a major setback when Massachusetts, which had banned tattooing, passed a law allowing tattoo parlors in the state. "Here we are supposed to be the bastion of medical science and we have just legalized this dangerous practice," says Seckel.

"Who is overseeing the process? We don't know if this equipment is properly sterilized. We don't know if the needles are disposed after a single use," says Seckel. "We don't allow nonmedical personnel to draw blood; why do we allow these people to pierce the skin?"

# Defending the Tattoo Profession

Macedonia, Ohio, tattoo artist Jerry Davis, 40, takes exception to Seckel's charges. Davis tells WebMD, "Dentists don't operate in hospitals. They learn all the necessary procedures for sterilization and disposal of hazardous materials. If they can learn it, who is to say that we can't learn it, too?"

Davis, who has operated a studio in the basement of an old schoolhouse for the last 15 years, says that he is interested in improving the image of tattoo artists and in improving health standards.

In his studio, where the walls are covered with thousands and thousands of tattoo designs, he points out that he has initiated some safety measures not required by Ohio law. For example, he insists that all his artists cover the tattoo machine—he objects to the term tattoo gun—in plastic to protect against blood splatter.

He says the entire tattoo machine cannot be placed in a sterilizer because it would be ruined. He does, however, sterilize the tubes that hold the pigment and the bar that holds the needles. He uses disposable needles "that are removed and disposed of in the presence of the customer."

Davis says he and the five artists he employs have all been tested for hepatitis B and have current vaccinations. They have not, however, been tested for hepatitis C, but he plans to change that. "I didn't know about this but now that I do, I will be tested. I would like to live to a ripe old age and to see my kids graduate from college, so I want to stay healthy," says Davis.

## Making Safe Choices

Husband and wife Hugh O'Donnell and Jenny Grospitch, both 30, say they are very happy with their 5-year-old tattoos. The Lakewood, Ohio couple says they did ask their tattoo artist about safety practices.

"We picked this place because it had a good reputation for safe practices and because the artist could do original designs," says Grospitch. She says she doesn't plan to get any more tattoos, but O'Donnell says he plans to get at least one more.

Asked about hepatitis C, both Grospitch and O'Donnell said they had never heard about it. However, Grospitch, O'Donnell, and Blackmarr all tell WebMD that they will now be tested for hepatitis C.

As O'Donnell puts it, "Of course, I'll get tested. It would be stupid not to. But I'm still going to get another tattoo."

If you have a tattoo and want to find out whether you've been exposed to hepatitis C, you can ask your doctor about getting your blood tested.

# How Tattoo Removal Works

Marshall Brain

By one physician's estimate, about 50 percent of people who get tattoos later regret them. Before the mid-1980s, persons wishing to have tattoos removed were faced with painful and often scar-inducing surgery. However, the advent of laser surgery revolutionized tattoo removal. Although lasers are not always 100 percent effective, the procedure has become much simpler and less painful. In the following viewpoint from his award-winning HowStuffWorks series, author Marshall Brain delves into the modern process of tattoo removal.

SO YOU DIDN'T BELIEVE YOUR MOM WHEN SHE said you'd regret getting that tattoo—the multicolored, fire-breathing dragon that starts at the small of your back, reaches up to your shoulder blades and wraps its orange flames around your biceps. Now, a mere seven years later, you have a shot at a terrific job in banking, still one of the more conservative businesses around, and you are concerned that your symbol of youthful self-expression could create problems in your new career.

Well, you're not alone. Tattoos have become part of American mainstream culture over the past couple of decades. Some estimate that more than 10 million Americans have at least one tattoo, and there are about 4,000 tattoo studios now in business in the United States. . . . One busy physician who specializes in tattoo removal—he's removed tattoos from some of the most famous tattoo artists—estimates that about 50 percent of those

■

who get tattoos later regret them. For years, these people had little recourse, and existing removal techniques were invasive (requiring surgery) and painful. But that's changing. . . .

*Can all tattoos be removed?* Most dermatologic surgeons caution that complete tattoo removal is not possible. Tattoos are meant to be permanent, so removing them is difficult. Few surgeons guarantee complete removal. Having said that, there are several methods of tattoo removal which have proven effective. The degree of remaining color variations or blemishes depends upon several factors, including size, location, the individual's ability to heal, how the tattoo was applied and how long it has been in place. For example, a tattoo applied by a more experienced artist may be easier to remove since the pigment was evenly injected in the same level of the skin. New tattoos may also be more difficult to remove than old ones.

Doctors say they can't predict the exact degree of removal because they generally don't know which of the 100 tattoo inks available today were used. (The U.S. Food and Drug Administration currently lists tattoo pigments as "color additives," which are intended only for application to the top layer of the skin.) Consult with a removal specialist—be sure to take a list of questions along.

*What methods are used for tattoo removal?* Before lasers became popular for tattoo removal starting in the late 1980s, removal involved the use of one or more of these often-painful, often scar-inducing surgeries:

- *Dermabrasion*, where skin is "sanded" to remove the surface and middle layers;
- *Cryosurgery*, where the area is frozen prior to its removal;
- *Excision*, where the dermatologic surgeon removes the tattoo with a scalpel and closes the wound with stitches (in some cases involving large tattoos, a skin graft from another part of the body may be necessary).

Although the procedures above are still used in certain cases today, *lasers (Light Amplification by the Stimulated Emission of Radiation)* have become the standard treatment for tattoo removal because they offer a bloodless, low risk, effective alternative with minimal side effects. Each procedure is done on an outpatient basis in a single or series of visits. Patients may or may not require topical or local anesthesia.

# How Lasers Remove Tattoos

As early as the 1960s, lasers had been developed for industrial uses. When researchers developed lasers that emitted wavelengths of light in short flashes called pulses, medical use became viable. These lasers can effectively remove tattoos with a low risk of scarring, according to the American Academy of Dermatology. The type of laser used to remove a tattoo depends on the tattoo's pigment colors. (Yellow and green are the hardest colors to remove; blue and black are the easiest.) The three lasers developed specifically for use in tattoo removal use a technique known as Q-switching, which refers to the laser's short, high-energy pulses:

- the Q-switched Ruby,
- the Q-switched Alexandrite,
- the Q-switched Nd: YAG, the newest system in this class of lasers and particularly advanced in the removal of red, blue and black inks.

Lasers work by producing short pulses of intense light that pass harmlessly through the top layers of the skin to be selectively absorbed by the tattoo pigment. This laser energy causes the tattoo pigment to fragment into smaller particles that are then removed by the body's immune system. Researchers have determined which wavelengths of light to use and how to deliver the laser's output to best remove tattoo ink. (If you're wondering if the laser might also remove normal skin pigment, don't worry. The laser selectively targets the pigment of the tattoo without damaging the surrounding skin.)

The unfortunate thing about tattoos is that both getting them and having them taken off can be uncomfortable. The impact of the energy from the laser's powerful pulse of light has been described as similar to getting hot specks of bacon grease on your skin or being snapped by a thin rubber band. . . . Because black pigment absorbs all laser wavelengths, it's the easiest to remove. Other colors, such as green, selectively absorb laser light and can only be treated by selected lasers based on the pigment color.

# Careful Preparation Is Required

In preparation for a laser procedure, doctors recommend that non-aspirin products, like Tylenol, be used for minor aches and pains prior to the procedure, because aspirin and non-steroidal anti-inflammatory agents such as Ibuprofen can produce pronounced bruising after treatment.

Further pre-treatment steps might include the application of a prescription anesthetic cream two hours before the laser session. It is wiped off just before laser surgery begins. (Some patients say they don't need this. Others prefer to have a local anesthetic injected into the tattoo prior to laser therapy. Pinpoint bleeding is sometimes associated with the procedure.) Then pulses of light from the laser are directed onto the tattoo, breaking up the pigment. Over the next few weeks, the body's scavenger cells remove pigment residues.

More than one treatment, which actually only takes minutes, is usually needed to remove an entire tattoo—the number of sessions depends on the amount and type of ink used and how deeply it was injected. Three-week intervals between sessions are required to allow pigment residue to be absorbed by the body.

## Aftercare and Side Effects

Following treatment, the doctor will apply an antibacterial ointment and dressing to the area, which should be kept clean with continued application of ointment as directed by your doctor. A shower or bath the day after treatment is okay, but the treatment area should not be scrubbed. Your skin might feel slightly sunburned for a couple of days and the treated area may remain red for a few weeks. The site might also form a scab, which should be handled gently. After healing, the site will gradually and continually fade.

Side effects of laser procedures are generally few but may include hyperpigmentation, or an abundance of color in the skin at the treatment site, and hypopigmentation, where the treated area lacks normal skin color. Other possible side effects include infection of the site, lack of complete pigment removal and a 5 percent chance of permanent scarring.

## The Expense of Tattoo Removal

Something to think about *before* you get that tattoo is the fact that having a tattoo removed is much more expensive than having one put on. Laser tattoo removal can range from several hundred dollars up into the thousands of dollars, depending upon the size, type and location of the tattoo and the number of visits required. More bad news is that medical insurance generally doesn't pay for tattoo removal, since it is considered aesthetic or cosmetic in nature. (Traumatic tattoos, which result from accidents or injury, are a different matter.)

Because this is a medical procedure, make sure to see a dermatologic surgeon who specializes in tattoo removal. Check with the American Society for Laser Medicine & Surgery or the American Society of Dermatologic Surgeons for a referral or ask your own doctor for the name of a specialist in your area. (Some tattoo parlors also provide tattoo removal services. Before you sign on, make sure the person doing the removal is a medical doctor who specializes in laser surgery! Tattoo removal, like tattoo application, carries with it the risk of infection and must be handled with extreme care.)

If you're a young person trying to escape gang life and you don't have the money to get those tell-tale tattoos removed, your tattoo doesn't have to last forever. . . . Some generous doctors, hospitals and local governments and civic groups around the nation are offering free tattoo removal to give teens like you a new chance at life.

# 3

**EXAMINING POP CULTURE**

# The Psychology of Body Modification

# The Social Psychology of Japanese Tattoos

Donald Richie

In his book *The Japanese Tattoo*, writer Donald Richie examines the significance of tattoos in relation to the collective psychology of Japanese society. The author greatly emphasizes the role tattoos play in providing communal identity. While tattoos are usually viewed as symbols of individuality in the West, they often serve in Japan as marks of initiation, candidacy, and membership in a person's chosen group. Although a tattoo solidifies a Japanese man's cultural identity, explains Richie, wearers do ascribe certain mythic and aesthetic qualities to their designs.

THE REASONS FOR BEING TATTOOED ARE AS VARious as are the tattoo designs themselves. Yet, like the designs, the reasons can also be codified. The resultant categories overlap and, to a certain extent, even disagree—and there are doubtless additional reasons not touched on here. In the main, however, those that I believe responsible for both the popularity of the tattoo and the form it took in Japan are indicated below.

## Badges of Initiation

When there is a masculine-group norm, one of the things the norm implies is that one is not a man until a certain act is performed or certain rituals are accomplished. Depending upon the group, this can be killing an animal, being sexually initiated, being allowed to drink and smoke, being permitted to drive, or merely being allowed to wear certain kinds of clothing.

Being tattooed qualifies as an initiatory act when it is part of a group norm—as it was among the Maoris, and as it continues to be among the sailors of some nationalities. In Japan such groups would include the gangsters and some workmen's groups; they would also have included the Japanese carpenters before World War II and the Edo-period firemen. The first tattoo, like the first long pants, is a badge of maturity. Its application marks a rite of passage from adolescence into manhood.

I know a small, cheap Japanese-style restaurant in Fukagawa, an old part of Tokyo. Here, several years back, they hired a new first cook who happened to be tattooed. He brought in a helper, also tattooed. In due time, the second cook, who had been working there longer than any of them, got himself tattooed. When they later hired a new kitchen boy, the tattooed three joined in attempting—eventually successfully—to make the youth have himself decorated. The reasons that they used were that one is not a man until one is tattooed, that it is unmanly (*otokorashikunai*) not to be tattooed, that he would still be a kid, *shombenkusai* (stinking of piss) until he was thus decorated. Once he began his tattoo, the chaffing ceased.

# Gaining Communal Membership

If everyone in a group is to do something, then all must actually do it, since the action defines the group. If the yakuza gangster is by definition tattooed, then all nascent yakuza must be tattooed before they can become real yakuza.

This is still true in Japan, a country much given to group manifestations of various kinds. Cooks still wear the kinds of hats cooks are supposed to wear; those going skiing or hiking dress up in full ski and hiking gear; company members wear the company badge in their buttonholes; and some artists still wear berets.

Such indications bind. They both create and identify the group. In Japan, more than in most countries, such groups are considered important and necessary. The language itself reflects (or creates) this. The word *nakama* (for which the dictionary gives such definitions as a set, a circle, a coterie) defines all those who are on the "inside," all the others being on the "outside." Any single Japanese belongs to many such nakama. These may be as loose as a hiking group or as tight as a family.

The manifestations suggest the strength of the bond: ski gear is obviously temporary, the company badge is more permanent, the tattoo, by its indelible nature, presumes a lifelong involvement with the nakama.

Groups where the tattoo is the membership badge do, thus, tend to have stronger ties, both formal and informal, than groups in which the indication is less permanent. The yakuza, for example, live in a very strong network of ceremonies, rituals, rites, and various codes of etiquette.

In the Fukagawa restaurant mentioned above, once all the people in the kitchen became tattooed, a true nakama was formed. The kitchen boy, formerly excluded from the amusements of the other three, was now included, and the four became inseparable.

## Seeking Candidacy

In the West it is accepted that the man who has himself tattooed is an individual, even a maverick—at any rate, a man who wants to set himself apart. While it is also true that tattooed men do tend to get together and form small groups upon occasion, it is nonetheless agreed that a tattooed Westerner is a loner and often an unaffiliated one. He chooses to be tattooed to set himself off, and he can do so because his country has no tattoo tradition.

But in a country such as Japan, which does have this tradition, no matter how submerged, the tattooed man is not an individual exercising his right to be different but a man who wants to join a group. Thus, in modern Japan, those who get tattooed are rarely loners. They are, rather, looking for some kind of membership. They want to belong to a nakama—even if it is only a nakama of those who are also tattooed.

As individuals, tattooed Japanese tend to be conservative, retiring, and much less individualistic than one might imagine. The violent and tattooed thug is a creature of popular imagination. The tattooed—yakuza or not—follow agreed-upon codes of behavior, are politically far to the right, and willingly conform to any required group standard.

Though the yakuza and the various workmen's groups use

the tattoo as a membership badge, there are in addition many individuals who are neither yakuza nor workmen, who belong to no such nakama, and who still get themselves tattooed.

There are many reasons for choosing to be tattooed, but in this context one of them would be that a highly visible badge mark indicates a willingness to join, a display of candidacy, even though there is no actual group that could be joined unless it be a tattoo club—and there are many.

I have often spoken with such people in public baths and saunas. After admiring their tattoos, I have then asked about their affiliations. They may belong to a group, but often they do not; they are sometimes the only ones in their company or store to be tattooed. They have many reasons for being tattooed, as one may imagine, but they usually mention that they live alone, have no particular family ties, have few obligations, and consequently (their words, not mine) thought that getting tattooed would be a good thing to do. In effect they have become their own nakama. They have also, I believe, indicated the need for such a nakama. Getting tattooed is thus a magical gesture—sincere because incapable of modification—that indicates that these individuals are by no means loners; that they are, rather, lonely.

## Marks of Cultural Definition

To be human is to be amorphous, unformed. Thus one of the main businesses of life is to make some sense out of the chaos of simply being human. In the West this often results in a set of opinions and character traits chosen by the individual himself. He decides he likes this and does not like that, that this is true and that is false, and thus builds up a coherent structure that he calls himself. Strong characters with strong personalities are thought well of in the West. This means that the man has successfully arranged his disorder and has imposed a proper and individualistic character upon himself.

In other countries, and Japan is one of them, a strong character is not well thought of. A man solving his own problems in this fashion creates problems for others. If he is so certain of what he likes and what he doesn't like, he will then not be able to adapt and compromise in the manner his culture finds both necessary and attractive. In Japan, therefore, people put themselves together differently. They do not structure any presumed inner man. Rather, they structure the outer.

The difference is often expressed collectively—hence all the nakama manifestations visible in Japan. These outward marks, all the badges and costumes, do not indicate any inner conviction, nor are they intended to. All necessary decisions are displayed on the surface; all the structuring that the West devotes to the inside is visible in Japan on the outside. Order is thus achieved in a way quite different, even opposite, from that common in Europe and North America.

At the same time there is the purely human urge to make the amorphous self into something certain, strong, unchanging. In the West this results in persons with strong and unvarying opinions who draw solace from their very consistency. They are able to reduce the world to a firmly opposed series of rights and wrongs.

# Indelible Symbols

In Japan a person with such a need has neither the training nor the example to be so opinionated. Rather, and often with equal rigor, he arranges his surface, his facade, in a manner he considers set, fixed, indubitable. Hence all the costume wearing, hence all the wearing of badges and other identifying emblems, and hence also, and in this sense tattoos.

A man who is fully tattooed is stable, unchanging. He has solidified his own skin and become that solid object, that permanent identity that all men in fear of the amorphous become. Indelibly dyed, unchanging, his skin supports him. Specifically, it defines him.

This means that his life is much less open to alternatives. This is a state toward which all men aspire. Alternatives—alternate ways of thought, for example—threaten the equilibrium of the structured man. In Japan tattoos remain as socially unrespectable as they once were in the West; there are many (a majority of) professions and avocations not open to a tattooed man. This means that his life is much simplified—it becomes manageable.

The tattooed man is thus one who needs this simplification. It does not follow that his thinking is codified to the extent common to the Western man of strong character and set opinions. Rather, it means that he need *not* codify his mind because his body has become codified. In both East and West, these various attempts at definition are based, further, upon a fear of the undefined.

## Tattoo as Talisman

The fear is specifically a fear of life—aimless, devouring, self-creating, monstrous life. It is not surprising, then, that death—safe, still, enclosed, impervious death—is very much present in the minds of such strong-seeming men.

In Japan, such things being open and openly acknowledged, tattooed men think and talk much about death. Some—the yakuza—are in a profession that traditionally assures an early demise. Others commonly tattooed, construction workers, for example, engage in work at least potentially dangerous. Like those nineteenth-century Frenchmen of whom one reads—*mort* written across the chest, a dotted line tattooed around the neck for the convenience of the guillotine—such Japanese sport their tattoos in the very face of death.

Nominally the talismanic tattoo is thought of as a preventative. It makes the wearer safe; it protects him. And this indeed is perhaps the function of the religious-symbol tattoos in Japan. But the matter is not quite so simple.

The tattoo may also be seen as a kind of death insurance. One of the minor indications of this is that one of the first things Japanese tattooed men bring up when asked about their reason for being tattooed is that after their demise their skin will be useful. They think of it as a kind of pelt that will be exhibited in a medical museum. One of the considered benefits is that the tattoo will be well regarded after their death. Or they will say that such institutions pay high prices for a skin, or that numbers of tattoo fanciers are waiting for the hide. Survivors could sell this valuable object, and hence wife and children could become financially independent. But, in fact, there are no such buffs, and though there is such a medical museum it has long ceased purchasing—if it ever did. And, in any event, such selling of a dead man's parts is illegal. Yet, none of this disturbs the hopeful myth.

One of the ways to read the myth is that tattooed men, in their efforts to communicate their strong feelings about death, will even vulgarize these into a concern for formaldehyde immortality or the financial advantage of the next of kin. No one, however, ever got tattooed for monetary reasons.

Another way to read the myth is to see it as an acknowledgment that unchanging permanence—in life, in death—represents a very satisfactory rebuttal to the demands of changing, chaotic life itself. In fact, being tattooed can be viewed as a kind of early demise. If life can be defined as amorphous and transient, then a permanent pattern, a sort of rigor mortis of the skin, can be seen as a kind of death.

Or as a kind of premature immortality, which amounts to much the same thing, since only after death can one become immortal. The tattooed man, much concerned with death, can be said to have removed death's sting by already, in his fashion, submitting himself to it, specifically by so limiting himself and his alternatives. . . .

## Beauty Marks

Tattooing is always thought by the tattooed to be cosmetic. Even if the aim is to intimidate through such decoration—as is partly the case with the yakuza—the patterns themselves are never thought of as ugly. Rather, they are beautiful and the wearer is aesthetically enhanced.

This is particularly true in Japan, a country where aesthetic appreciation and common machismo are no strangers, and where tattooing has become an art—where, indeed, tattoos *are* beautiful. But the next question is: beautiful to and for whom?

Here one often encounters a medical-museum type of answer. Tattoos are irresistible to the opposite sex; one of the reasons men tattoo themselves is to become attractive to women. There is, of course, some truth in this. One remembers the Tokugawa-period stories of tattooed courtesans and tattooed roughs, and their being particularly desirable lovers. Nowadays, however, when things are quite different, the tattooed still present the same answer: it makes them attractive—specifically, sexually attractive.

This is indeed an answer common in all countries, and there are probably a certain number of women who might consider tattooed men particularly desirable, reeking as they do of society's idea of the ultramasculine. In Japan, however, the number of such women must be small indeed. Japanese women, still largely subscribing to the male idea of the world, are even more stringent than Japanese men in observing social norms. And the tattoo is outside that norm. . . .

I do not believe that Japanese women find tattoos attractive. If anything, they find them the opposite. Certainly those few women who get themselves tattooed are either the wives or companions of tattooers, in which case they often serve as his scribble board; or whose husbands or lovers are tattooed, in which case a special interest is involved. A certain amount of verification for my view comes from tattooed men themselves. The unmarried tattooed man, having said that he had himself decorated for romantic reasons, will often, since he has now brought the subject up, then begin to complain about his bad luck in failing to meet the sort of woman whom he presumably had himself decorated for.

## Narcissistic Motives

It becomes apparent that the object for whom the beautification is endured is different from that stated. Specifically, as has been earlier implied, a man is tattooed for his own sake. In addition, and to a lesser degree, he has himself tattooed for the admiration and envy of other men.

The prime reason is thus narcissistic—that well-known erotic feeling aroused by one's own body. It does not follow, however, that the secondary reason is therefore homosexual, though the mores of yakuza and workers include the homosexual to a degree uncommon in the West. The primary eroticism aroused by the tattoo is autoeroticism. . . .

These, then, are some of the reasons Japanese men have found for going to the expense, time, and pain of acquiring tattoos. The result is that very often the man himself becomes a work of art—an object the parts of which conform to a principle creating a harmony that cannot but be aesthetically pleasing and psychologically satisfying.

# Body Modifications Heal the Mind/Body Split

Maureen Mercury

In the following excerpt from her book *Pagan Flesh-works: The Alchemy of Body Modification*, author Maureen Mercury points to the mind/body split as a primary motivational factor for getting a tattoo or body piercing. The author explains that seventeenth century French philosopher René Descartes' famous dictum, "I think, therefore I am," asserted the primacy of mind over body and set in motion the dissociation of feeling experience. Modern society's reliance on mental concentration and acuity has only suppressed the body senses even more, according to Mercury. She argues that tattooing and body piercing can awaken sensate functioning and heal the mind/body split.

NO EXPLANATION OF THE RISE AND PROLIFERA-tion of modern fleshworks would be sufficient without an exploration of the roots of the mind/body split in Western consciousness.

Contemporary life has us spending many of our waking hours seated in a car, seated in a classroom, seated and watching television, seated and working on a computer, and seated enjoying movies, sports, and other forms of entertainment. All these activities do require concentration and mental acuity. Some of them even require developed motor skills. But none engages the entire body in an integrated fashion. None offers

■

any connection to the natural nonmechanistic sensory world. It is not surprising then that we hear the silent scream of the neglected and starving sensate body.

The pagan psyche is longing to integrate thinking functions with the physical, sensate body. This is difficult in modern times because the physical body is increasingly becoming displaced, or dissociated. The essence of a pagan psyche is rooted in place. We see ourselves in relation to others. We contextualize ourselves through our lineage, our ancestors, and our bloodlines. We need to feel part of larger social entities: families, communities, nations. The advent of cyberspace has created a rootless, placeless society, accessed by the seated and thinking. One's place is nowhere or anywhere. We communicate through an e-mail address and locate ourselves on personal home pages. The physical body never interacts with anyone.

A result of this statelessness is psychic and physical numbness. Tattooing, piercing, implanting, and branding are means of jump-starting sensate functioning that has lost its capacity for feeling.

## A Revolution of Logic

A short visit to the seventeenth century will help us understand why so much of our daily lives is spent in a seated and thinking position, how we became so split off from our natural body rhythms, and how we became so alienated from the natural world. The seventeenth century was a turbulent time in history. We have a healthy distance now, but the people of that age had the foundations of their beliefs swept out from under them. . . .

In 1637 French philosopher, mathematician, and scientist René Descartes (1596–1650) was formulating a philosophical position vis-à-vis the world around him that would have consequences far greater than he could have ever dreamed. He published the work *Discourse on Method*, in which he attempted to apply mathematical methods to philosophy. In the study of physical science, he rejected traditional methods of experimentation and relied on rationalization, logic, and mathematics.

Descartes is best known for his work *Meditationes de prima philosophia* (published in 1641), in which he wrote the statement, "Cogito, ergo sum"; I think, therefore I am." This statement declared the primacy of ego perception, placing the ego at the center of the universe, thus launching us into the scientific morass in which we find ourselves today. . . .

With the adoption of this philosophy, gone was the pagan vision of the world with its multilayered meanings based on what Descartes considered unreal, unreliable, and unprovable perceptive tools of fantasy, intuition, and imagination.

# Splitting Mind from Body

Here is the mind/body split at its source. Ego (mind) is on one side and is understood as a total thinking system, including consciousness and subjective experience. The rest of the world—which constitutes the entire physical universe, including plants, animals, stones, stars, and the physical body!—is on the other side, separate from the ego. In the Cartesian vision, the entire physical universe is seen as inanimate, mechanistic, devoid of autonomous feelings, and, as such, is essentially composed of constructs operating on autopilot. . . .

Look at your daily activities. How many of them keep you split off from the natural world? How many jobs allow intuitive hunches and imaginative, unproven solutions to problems? How many jobs have you sitting and thinking? There is a premium, in our culture, assigned to those who can live within this paradigm. Schools are designed for seated thinkers. High paying jobs are designed for seated thinkers. But we are embodied souls, with a core need for integration of mind and body. And as we have seen, what is repressed, what is pushed away in the psyche, will reassert itself and shout until it is heard.

The adoption of the Cartesian philosophy " I think, therefore I am" has led us to the place of technological advancement in which we live today. The cost of that statement has been enormous. In the devaluation of animals and nature we are witnessing the advent of apocalypse. The devastation of global ecosystems and the extinction of many animal species are easily observable phenomena. What is not so easy to observe, at first glance, is the damage an egocentric philosophy has done to those of us in the West who live under the Cartesian paradigm. This paradigm has split us off from nature, and from the honoring of imagination, and by extension, has split us off from the sacred matrix of connection to the cosmos. And we are paying with our souls.

The pain of this separation from the sacred web is driving many back to the physical body for healing. It is an instinctive, intuitive movement. A movement designed to reanimate forgotten and deadened areas of the psyche through a somatic, or body-felt, experience.

## The Initiated Body

Tattooing, piercing, branding, and implanting the body are, at a basic level, rites of initiation that attempt to heal the mind/body split. They integrate the impulse to get a modification (whether conceived consciously or unconsciously) into a living body part through the ensuing sensation of the marking.

Initiatory experiences are threshold phenomena that move the intent of the ego from a former state of being to a larger, more expansive state. When one engages in a threshold crossing, the gates between our levels of consciousness—ego, personal unconscious, and collective unconscious—swing open, if only for a moment. An initiation through body modification creates a sensate threshold crossing, testing one's endurance for pain, while leaving the initiate with a badge of the crossing. This form of initiation gives physical witness to significant life passages—a permanent marking or manifestation of a life-altering experience or transition.

The human need for significant threshold crossings is an archetypal desire. We long for a measure of our strength, courage, or endurance—it is inherent in our souls. In ancient times the movement from adolescence to manhood was accompanied by elaborate rituals to mark this most dramatic transition in a man's life. The rituals were designed to ensure the initiate's full participation and cognizance of the significance of the passage. Initiation into the society of men marked the irreversible direction that a man would take as he assumed his role within his tribe.

The capacity of a body modification initiation to produce a psychologically transformative experience is based on the level of consciousness with which the participant enters the process. The greater the level of consciousness, the greater the psychological transformation. . . .

The ritual of a threshold crossing is vital to our personal growth and is often sought at times of life transition. It is only through such transition rituals that we become who we are meant to be. This life process, this personal becoming, [psychologist Carl] Jung termed *individuation*. Often this drive, which originates in the realm of the collective unconscious, has little to do with what your ego thinks you will become. Jung believed that this urge was so strong that it forced shadow material to consciousness and had the power to shape one's destiny.

# Marking Rites of Passage

According to Arnold van Gennep in *The Rites of Passage*, rites of passage can be subdivided into rites of separation (such as funerals), transition rites (initiation, pregnancy, or engagement), and rites of incorporation (marriage). It is the transition rites of initiation that particularly pertain to body marking and modification. In indigenous cultures, a transitional rite of passage is marked by three distinct psychic states: separation, liminality, and reaggregation.

In the separation stage of initiatory rituals of tribal cultures, adolescent boys are physically abducted from their villages and taken to sacred places away from that which is familiar. The point of the mock abduction is to separate them from the world of women (the world of their youthful innocence) and return them as men. . . .

In our modern culture, there is no clear ritualized separation from parents, loving friends or partners, and the rest of the community when one is ready to cross the threshold into adulthood. In our culture, those ready to make the transition must create their own acts of separation and initiation—often performing these acts alone with no support structure. Tattoos, piercings, and other forms of fleshworks have become a common modern initiation. If the initiate is under the legal age for fleshworks, lying and breaking the law creates an additional separation from the community. The process of getting a tattoo or piercing becomes the goal of the initiation: crossing a threshold of body sensation sometimes perceived as pain. The marking is worn as the proof of that crossing and of the accompanying transition.

By separating from the rest of the community, the initiate moves into a sacred space where linear time is temporarily suspended. This phase is termed liminality, or liminal time. In tribal cultures, this is the time when the myths and mysteries of creation are taught to the neophytes. In liminality, the *sacra* (sacred knowledge) is passed on. Tribal elders and adepts are responsible for the teaching. They are "those who have gone before," or those who have been initiated themselves.

In our modern culture, initiates enter into liminal space at the moment they enter the studio with a tattoo, piercing, branding, implant, or scarification in mind. Sadly, the myths and mysteries of our Western tribe are only revealed to the extent that the artist administering the marking is conscious of the significance of the initiatory process.

In the tattoo or piercing studio, as in traditional tribal rites of passage, the natural world is forgotten as the chosen body part receives the marking. One has the impression that time is temporarily suspended. At this moment, as in tribal cultures, the initiates are mythically linked to the marked ancestors who have preceded them and to those yet unborn who will search for their own form of threshold crossing.

The reemergence from the liminal stage, when suspended time begins again to move in a linear fashion, is called ludic recombination. In an initiation through body modification, this is the closing moment of the ritual, when the wound is complete and bandaged and the novice receives aftercare instructions.

## Symbols of Transition

The last phase of a ritual threshold crossing is the reaggregation into the community. At this stage, the neophyte returns to the tribe a changed man, or in contemporary society, the initiate leaves the studio wearing the badge of transition and returns to the profane world with new experiential knowledge.

In the transitional rites of passage of tattooing, piercing, branding, scarification, or implanting, the body has served as the vehicle for a potential psychic transformation. The marked individuals are removed from the common mass of humanity and reincorporated into a group defined by their having crossed a particular threshold. The crossing is not a simple one, even if the decision to become marked has been arrived at with little conscious thought. The choice to engage a sensate threshold, in addition to a psychological one, places those initiates within the ancient tradition of using the body as a vehicle for the search for ecstatic experience.

## An Ecstatic Quest

Ecstasy is perceived in the psyche as an encounter with the numinous or divine. This encounter is marked by one's sense of the ineffable, the unknowable, or the religious. A construct of purely subjective experience, one's encounter with the numinous, or the divine, makes sacred events that for others may appear profane or irrelevant. For those who choose body modification and the continuum of sensations that accompany the work as their path for an encounter with a sense of the divine, ecstasy is not guaranteed. We can enhance our chances of ecstatic union with the sacred by observing those who have mastered the quest for ecstasy: the shamans.

No group of individuals has so completely mastered techniques of ecstasy as those who practice shamanism. That the study and practice of core shamanism is being revived today is no accident. After centuries of living with a scientific paradigm and witnessing the eco-soulular destruction wrought by such, a backlash wave of interest in inner symbols of meaning is asserting itself. Discovery of archetypal symbols and patterns of resonance with the soul prompt a desire to understand and explore one's connection to larger archetypal patterns of the world soul. Core shamanism is a path for these explorers.

*Shaman* is a word from the Tungus people of Siberia that has been adopted by anthropologists to mean many different things: witch doctor, medicine man, sorcerer, wizard, seer, and magician. The word *shaman*, however, does not carry the prejudicial overtones that the preceding words do. Also, not all magicians, medicine men, and so forth, are shamans. [In his book *The Way of the Shaman*, author Michael Harner writes,] "A shaman is a man or woman who enters an altered state of consciousness—at will—to contact and utilize an ordinarily hidden reality in order to acquire knowledge, power, and to help other persons. The shaman has at least one, and usually more, 'spirits' in his personal service.". . .

The journey to divine realms demands that practicing

shamans move out of ordinary reality to nonordinary reality, while in an altered state of consciousness. This is not a drug-induced trip. Very particular drumming patterns serve as the springboard for this altered state. To distinguish states of consciousness, we will use the abbreviations SSC (for the altered consciousness of Shamanic State of Consciousness) and OSC (for the Ordinary State of Consciousness, or how we operate in everyday or ordinary reality).

A prerequisite for understanding a shamanic journey from ordinary to nonordinary realms is the acceptance of a principle basic to indigenous people: there is no difference between what we imagine and what is real. This principle directly contradicts Cartesian thought and challenges our Western scientific assumptions. For those of us raised in the West, the lack of distinction between reality and imagination is a hard concept to swallow. But for indigenous people, what they imagine to happen is as real as what their ego perceives as happening.

The imaginary realm exists as a valid universe in nonordinary reality, and the ego realm exists as a valid universe in ordinary reality. The two realms are equal and exist as parallel: one visible to the eye, one hidden from plain sight and visible only to the inner eye. Following a pagan vision that there are many facets to the psyche, and that external divinities and internal personal gods reflect those facets, these parallel universes are equally animated. Animals have the ability to convey messages in ordinary reality, although it takes some work to decipher their messages. In contrast, the nonordinary world, to one in SSC, is animated to the point where animals are plain-speaking guides and helping spirits.

## Accessing Formless Energy

Where practicing shamans and people engaging in modern fleshworks meet at a matrix is their respective desire to experience ecstasy. While shamanic practitioners transcend the body, modern initiates move through the body—marking images, piercing holes, branding designs, and implanting sacred symbols. Intense sensation, or sensation perceived as prolonged pain, is desired by those engaging in fleshworks because at the moment when one surrenders and transcends the pain, there may open a realm of consciousness that Jung called *the psychoid*.

Ego is the outer skin of the onion. As we peel away that skin, the next closest layer is the personal unconscious. Deeper still is the unconscious of world soul with its bubbling and seething archetypal images and charges: the collective unconscious. After peeling away the skins of the onion, we see the core. Now throw the core away and take a deep breath. In the whiff of stinging vapors that bring tears to your eyes is the realm of psychoid archetypes.

As with the vaporous odor of the onion, psychoid archetypes have no form. They are charged but formless. We sense them but cannot see evidence of them in images. Although fundamental core psychic energies, they are unknowable to ego. They are always just on the edge of consciousness—a flash of light seen from the corner of your eye, a deep sense of knowing without proof, an unprovoked cold chill running down your spine.

Because we are talking about primary forms of pure energy, they exist in an undifferentiated form. The typical rules of archetypes do not apply. Psychoid archetypes have no polarity. Pleasure and pain, weak and strong, positive and negative, do not exist at this level of consciousness.

## Experiencing the Divine

Ecstasy is felt when all of the floodgates of consciousness are open and the charge of psychoid contents is allowed to move freely. Some people liken these moments to touching God. There is no doubt that our physical bodies are infused with numinosum. Just as there is no doubt that our psyches perceive these moments as sacred, in their depth of feeling.

Practicing shamans have the ability to open the floodgates of consciousness at will. They have the ability to connect to energetically charged psychoid archetypes and to feel a body sense of the divine.

Contemporary Western people, for the most part, do not practice core shamanism. It is antithetical to our cultural and religious orientation to even think that we can contact any divine entity outside of a religious institution. Besides, most of us delegate that mission to clergy and take messages from

Heaven secondhand. However, those who engage in body rituals of initiation want to make that connection themselves.
The connection is the goal of the process. Whether one is
conscious or unconscious of that goal, psychoid archetypes are
invoked when one transcends the polarity of a pleasure/pain
continuum and receives a fleshwork.

# Tattoed People as Taboo Figures

Kelly Rothenberg

Seeking to better understand how tattoos function in society, researcher Kelly Rothenberg interviewed fourteen people—some tattooed, others not—at Florida State University in 1996. Rothenberg discovered a subculture marked by negative lore and extreme individualism, a "folk group" that is often viewed in opposition to mainstream society. She also discovered, however, that the popularization of tattoos in the media and among celebrities has begun to relax the characterization of the practice as taboo. Rothenberg summarized her interviews in the following article for *Body Modification Ezine*.

*"Everybody wants to see the pictures, and yet nobody wants to see them."*                    Ray Bradbury—*The Illustrated Man*

THERE USED TO BE A TIME, BACK IN THE DAYS OF P.T. Barnum, when circuses traveled from town to town. There were always crowds for the usual sights—the elephants, the clowns, the strongman, et cetera—but it was at the Freak Show where you could see the Bearded Lady, the Human Skeleton, or perhaps the Elephant Man and, if you were really good boys and girls, you might get to see [what writer Stephen King describes as] "the tattooed man with the tail of a dragon curled around his burly neck like a fabulous hangman's noose." Freak shows are uncommon nowadays, but there is still the urge to stare at the crippled person, or the person with some other sort of oddity about them. People with tattoos willingly

■

go out and place themselves in this center of attention, acting as modern-day taboo breakers and crossing a line that most of us would just as soon leave alone, that final boundary between societal acceptance and ostracism.

## Overcoming Stereotypes

This article will not retell the stories I collected, or try to analyze the symbolism each individual tattoo represents, though each was given to me readily by the people I interviewed. Instead, I focused on how society reacts to this folk group, and how this folk group reacts and thinks about itself. Why is this a folk group? Because the people who have gotten tattooed share a common knowledge that others outside the group—people without tattoos—have no access to. Instead, these outsiders have to draw from a pool of preconceived notions about this folk group, including notions about drug use, being a member of a gang, or some other deviant aspect about them. There is always a grain of truth in stereotypes such as these and they may apply to some people, but stereotypes never apply to everyone.

To better understand the whole concept of taboos, it would be good to start with a working definition of what a taboo is. The one that I like best is by Lewis Spence, who says that a taboo is "a Polynesian word meaning 'prohibited' and signifying a prohibition enforced by religious or magical power, which has come to be applied to similar usages among savage peoples all over the world. *Taboo* [italics from source quote], or prohibition is enforced in the cases of sacred things and unclean things." Notice the word "unclean." Unclean denotes something negative and dirty, and tattoos are thought of by many in this same way, usually by people without tattoos. For example, Rickie and Lynn (no last names provided) hate the idea of tattoos with a passion. In Rickie's case it's because her sister, who lives in Texas, "has two tattoos . . . and now, she hates them." She goes on to say that it was "one of those druggie . . . things." Deloyd Loveless has seen the results of a bad tattoo first-hand. His friend, who wanted a tattoo in the first place, got something that looked like "a lopsided tire with a pair of wings that was barely outlined . . . Something about 'Wings On Wheels.'" Someone Francis Moore knows tried to get the lyrics to Jimi Hendrix's "Voodoo Child" tattooed on his back, but because the tattooist left out a couple of "O"s the person ended up with "Vodo Child . . . So he had it all covered up with clouds and everything." Vern Howe's friend Kotkie actually did get drunk (as is often the stereotype) and woke up to find, "Fumio, I Love You," tattooed on his rear end. As a side note, nobody I interviewed made the decision to get a tattoo while under the influence of alcohol, contrary to popular lore. They were also all educated college students, as opposed to being "people who's not quite evolved enough yet," as Deloyd Loveless puts it.

## The Negative Lore of Tattoos

It seems that each little piece of negative lore about tattoos has other lore implications associated with it. Lynn says, "If you have a tattoo, you ride a motorcycle," and Rickie finishes, "If you ride a motorcycle, you're not a feminine kind of woman." Along with seeing people with bad tattoo experiences, they have also had this reinforced by their parents; in Rickie's case, her father. "My father told me if I ever got one that he would peel the skin off." Bikers have their own particular tattoo lore which, according to Jed Wired, may not be "associated with anyone in particular, except that it's just supposed to mean you've killed someone." This appears to be a well-rooted piece of lore, because I heard many of the same things from a lot of different people. Jamie Sadler says that if you're in a gang and "you have a tattoo of a tear on your cheek, it means you've killed someone in a gang fight." Amy Schneider says, "It's also a biker's thing to tattoo a spider web on your elbow if you've killed someone."

Tattoos are also associated with broken hearts, usually involving someone getting their lover's/spouse's name tattooed on their body, only to end up with the relationship eventually falling apart and the person stuck with a tattoo of a bad memory. Charlie, someone who worked for Deloyd's father, removed his wife's name himself. "I'm no longer married now. So I have scrubbed her off of my arm with a heated knife blade!" Lynn plays soccer with a friend who tattooed her boyfriend's name "across her thigh . . . and broke up with him three days after she got the tattoo." A lady Gina Mavigliano saw had a tattoo of the year "1974" on her arm, which her husband had tattooed on her arm on their wedding night while he was drunk. "Since then she's been divorced, but that little tattoo has been a great reminder of a mistake that she obviously once made."

Francis Moore told me about the skinhead with "the opening sentence from *Mein Kampf* on the back of his head," and Vern Howe told me about the Bitch of Buchenwald, where the commandant's wife (Frau Koch) had people's tattooed skin made into lamp shades. "She would take the skin and then she would cure it and . . . she'd make beautiful lamp shades and everything out of people's skin." In the book *Hitler's Death Camps: The Sanity of Madness*, Konnilyn G. Feig notes that "one piece of skin that struck her [Frau Koch's] fancy had the words 'Hansel and Gretel' tattooed on it." With stories like these, it's little surprise that tattoos have such a horrendous type of lore surrounding them.

## Personal Statements and Rites of Passage

So, with all these horror stories about tattoos, why do people still get them? The reasons seem to fit into two main categories. The first one is a way for them to state their personal beliefs, which is also the reason why someone chooses to get a particular design tattooed on their body. In Scott Brightwell's case, it was a way of reinforcing his belief in the martial arts customs that he had been taught. "It's part of the philosophy I learned along the way, and it's just something that really struck me as a nice way to live, a nice little thing to live by." Amy Schneider is a feminist, and her tattoo reflects this. "Here was a statement that I could say, 'I'm in control of my own body. I do whatever I want with it . . . I want a reminder that I believe these things, and I thought they were this important.'" Jed Wired is a self-admitted hippie, and designed a peace symbol that included the initials of two close friends, and the Greek letters Lambda Sigma Delta. "It's kind of a joke," Jed says about the Greek letters. "It's just translating to English lettering." If you do that, you get the letters LSD, which is also associated with sixties hippiedom. More importantly, though, the tattoo "was a friendship thing. There were three of us, and we got the same thing in the same spot." Although he isn't as close as he once was with these people, he doesn't regret getting the tattoo because it still reflects his other beliefs. Bill O'Berry says of the reason he got a tattoo, "I wanted something that couldn't be taken away from me. No matter what, I could go all the way to my grave and it would still be with me."

The other reason I discovered for getting a tattoo fits in very closely with [writer] Laura Makarius' study of ritual clowns. For some people, getting a tattoo is a symbol for a rite of passage that no longer takes place in today's society. Troy Steiner, an avant garde dancer from New York and other places, says, "I feel here, especially in America, there are no more rites of passage anymore . . . and you have to design your own." It's appropriate that Troy got his tattoo on his twentieth birthday, since birthdays were often associated with maturation and initiation rites in many Indian groups. Francis Moore also feels that "it's a rite of passage still, you know. People don't really talk about it that much anymore." Joining a select group usually involves some sort of initiation. To join the Russian club might require taking the Russian language. To become a taboo figure involves breaking a code that society holds above all else. To a lot of people, decorating the body with art is such a taboo. "It's degrading and defacing your body," says Deloyd Loveless. Brian Ravetta adds, "But for me it's sort of a religious thing . . . Would you go and spray graffiti on your temple? And I believe your body is a temple to God."

## A Mark of Taboo

[In her book *Ritual Clowns and Symbolic Behavior,* writer] Laura Makarius, when discussing the backwards behavior of North American Indians, writes, "Thus the evidence shows that backward speech . . . is associated with the violation of taboo in order to underline it, bring it out clearly and mark its author as a 'contrary' person, exceptional and opposed to the other members of society." Getting a tattoo is the same thing: it marks you as someone different from society, different from everybody else. Stephanie [no last name provided] says a tattoo "marks a person separately . . . It sets me apart." In a society that is increasingly conformist in many ways, other people are trying to find other ways to set themselves apart from the crowd. They want to reaffirm their uniqueness to themselves and others, and tattoos are one way to do it. I wouldn't say this applies to everybody, but it applies to some people. In some cultures, in order to fit in you have to have a tattoo. Brian Ravetta's friend from England has several tattoos that would probably be considered obscene in America, including one "that grows and will occasionally fire." Why such an obscene tattoo? "He's from the Northeast of England, which is an extremely hard area . . . where . . . men are men. And tattooing is part of the culture." If he hadn't gotten tattooed, his life would have been even harder because he didn't fit in. In that part of the world, then, the taboo would have been being arrogant enough not to get a tattoo, and not to conform with that tradition.

Brian's friend has sexually suggestive tattoos. It's not surprising that tattoos and sexuality—both taboo subjects—should have merged at one point. Like the tattooed man at the freak show, most people love to hear dirty jokes, or jokes with deviant behavior in it, but won't usually admit it. The few dirty jokes I collected were from Vern Howe. . . . Vern's tattoo jokes combine several types of ideas found in sexual humor. The story about "Dot," as I call it, combines the idea of tattooing your lover's name on your body with penis size. "When the thing gets long and hard, it spells CHRISTINA JORGENSON." Obviously sexual humor wouldn't be possible without reference to either the sexual act or the sexual organs. In Vern's other joke, this time the female pubic area is used, being referred to as "Grizzly Adams" and showing that humor, like the people who get tattoos, has no gender barriers. There are also gender stereotypes involved in the humor. The male of the "Dot" joke is shown as getting a tattoo as a noble gesture to remember someone he loves. The woman in the "Grizzly Adams" joke does it strictly for vanity, which is something women are accused of quite often.

## Changing Attitudes

So, are the taboos breaking down? Troy Steiner feels that tattoos have become "somewhat fashionable, if you will." In his case, as an avant garde dancer, he considers his tattoo an asset. While the arts are generally more open-minded about such things, there are still people in society who keep the tattoo lore alive, mainly the mass media industry of television, movies and literature. Both Deloyd Loveless and Gina Mavigliano feel that these have contributed to people's notions about tattoos. While it may not be intentional, many of these sources themselves still draw from the lore that's available to them for their material.

In Thomas Harris' novel *The Silence of the Lambs*, the psychopath Buffalo Bill has two tattoos on his left hand and one on his chest. According to popular lore, if he's a psychopath, then he must have tattoos. Drawing upon this negative cultural lore about tattoos helps make the atmosphere of the movie even more sinister, because everyone recognizes the symbols for what they are. As a further note of emphasis, Buffalo Bill was the only character with tattoos in the entire story. Even Brant Parker's comic strip "The Wizard of Id" made the idea of a blind date even worse by giving her tattoos on her lips. Note the date of the strip: October 16, 1991. We consider ourselves an open-minded society, yet old preconceptions still pop up. As the older generation passes on, though, the more open ideas of the younger generation will predominate.

Everything is cyclical: fashion, politics, and even attitudes towards tattoos. Gina Mavigliano describes people's attitudes towards tattoos as going from "representing honor, like for the war . . . Then I think people came to think of them as kind of dirty . . . 'oh, only lower class people have tattoos,'" back to the mainstream of college campuses. "It just seems like a lot of younger people, college students that I know, have gotten tattoos," she says. Both Gina and Troy have accurately described what is happening in this lore group. Look at all the media personalities—Cher, Julia Roberts, Roseanne—that have gotten tattoos. People see other well-known people getting them and decide that it wouldn't be so bad to get one themselves. If they do decide to get one for whatever reasons, though, they want it to be unique, so they either design their own tattoo or let the artist add his own flair to it. Scott Brightwell says of his, "This was taken from a book, yet it's not a direct copy. It has the design of the tattoo artist in it; his own inflections on the gun."

# From Taboo to Mainstream

The barriers are breaking down because more and more people have crossed the line of taboo, and shown that nothing bad has happened. When I did the research for this article . . . at Florida State University, I was honestly surprised to find the number of people I did who weren't bikers or punkers or some other cliché. I was drawing from the same lore pool that everyone else had, fed by the media. I think that once things become unstigmatized they can never go back to being completely stigmatized again. The taboos haven't completely broken down yet, though they are slowly weakening.

What was once taboo is now becoming mainstream, and in fact has become so mainstream that body art has already moved on to the next level with body piercing, which will also continue to push the mainstream acceptance envelope until either something else comes along to surpass it, or society snaps backwards to ultra-conservancy once again. It won't snap back completely, but the interest will eventually wane. Tattoos are not a point of fashion for the majority of the people who have them, but to the outsiders looking in to the group it appears to be this way. Once their fascination to stare dies down, however, tattooing and other body art will slip back into the background. Society doesn't treat people with tattoos as freaks anymore, but even so, "there is something so attractive about freaks, yet something so forbidden and appalling." I think we all feel the attraction to see, but just don't want to be caught staring. If we don't look, though, we'll never learn to see past the barrier.

# Body Art Is More than Mere Adornment

Kim Hewitt

In the following excerpt from her book *Mutilating the Body: Identity in Blood and Ink*, writer Kim Hewitt argues that body modification possesses a significance greater than mere adornment. Hewitt writes that actual pain of getting a tattoo or a body piercing carries importance, marking the process as an initiatory experience. She also notes that participants are in effect stigmatizing themselves in order to demonstrate their defiance against societal norms and to openly claim a public identity. The author wrote this book in response to her struggle with self-scarification in her youth.

TATTOOING AND PIERCING ARE NOT JUST ADORN- ments added to the body surface like jewelry or cosmetics— they penetrate the flesh. Piercing is a quick process followed by several weeks of tenderness while healing. Tattooing is a tedious, painful process followed by a period of transformation in which the wound heals and the redesigned body emerges. These adornments, like self-starvation and self-cutting, accrue significance from both the process of physical transformation and the final product. . . .

## The Significance of Pain

Many cultures attach social status to body alterations and consider pain a crucial element for imparting meaning to body al-

Excerpted from *Mutilating the Body: Identity in Blood and Ink*, by Kim Hewitt (OH: Bowling Green State University Popular Press, 1997). Copyright © 1997 by Bowling Green State University Popular Press. Reprinted with permission.

teration. Yoruban scarification is not only considered aesthet-ically pleasing but announces the marked individual's fortitude and ability to endure pain. A Yoruban woman acquires her markings when she is old enough to marry and accept the painful ordeal of childbirth. [In his article "Beauty and Being," researcher Henry Drewal points out that] her *kolo* cicatrices [scars] "exhibit her willingness to bear pain. . . . Aesthetic value is bound up with the value of endurance and the willingness to bear discomfort to accomplish a greater good." Tiv women re-mark on the ability of scarification to indicate masculinity and the desire to withstand pain in order to be attractive. . . .

Withstanding the pain of tattooing and other body alter-ations is also significant in American culture. The tattooee or piercee, like any initiate, vulnerably awaits the pain and new sta-tus the procedure will impart. Enduring pain is often considered crucial to gender constructions and demonstration of toughness. Although some tattooees have a difficult time bearing the pain, others see it as a "good pain." Part of the pleasure of a tattoo is the macho implication of being able to bear the pain, and during the 1950s and 1960s getting a tattoo was a common rite of pas-sage into adulthood for many young men. Still today, withstand-ing the tedious and painful process with bravado may be required to gain membership in a youth gang, or to demonstrate rebellion against authority. College fraternities may require members to get tattooed or pierced as a sign of their loyalty.

[In her article "Do Unto Others," writer Jan Seeger quotes] one tattoo artist with many tattoos [who] connects the pain of the process with the pleasure of creativity. "It's a strange metaphor to say that pain is like an orgasm—but it is in a way. And it's like labor too . . . to go through this pain to create a thing, to get it out of you. The design is inside of you, it just wants to get out." The creative expression of identity is enhanced by the feeling of "aliveness" that accompanies the pain of the process for many people. "This sense of existing, of feeling, of enjoying life, [comes] to many with the touch of the needle," [writes Samuel Steward in his book *Bad Boys and Tough Tattoos*]. The prolonged pain produces euphoria for many, and pain is also a meaningful and enjoyable element of the piercing process for some piercees as well as people who indulge in body branding or scarification.

# Traditional Marks of Transition

Individuals who tattoo and pierce imbue the body with narcissistic or magico-religious powers to confirm identity and connect them to either a deeper self-awareness, a social group, or a vision of integration with the cosmos. Similar to the way in which the self-mutilator or anorectic physically demarcates a change in self-awareness and interaction with the surrounding milieu, an individual who chooses to self-mark physically confirms a change in status. The "badge of admission" may carry personal meaning as well as a message of affiliation with a religion, one other person, a community, a youth gang, a fraternity, a military organization, or any specific group. The complexity of the action lies in the fact that the confirmation of identity is based on distancing the self from a large nonmarked portion of the population. . . .

The change in status, similar to the self-mutilator's change in tension level and temporary "cure" of feelings of fragmentation, sometimes signifies an attempt to overcome a distressing experience and alter self-concept. Other times, especially with tattooing, the experience is more of an aesthetic than an emotional transformation. Tangible transformation sometimes approaches a mystical experience. Approximating [sociologist Michel] Thevoz's theory of the ability of masks to induce "sacred awe," one piercee commented, "I enjoyed the mysterious separation from the everyday." Another noted, "I think my [piercing] jewelry magically transforms a piece of flesh into a work of art." Marking the body is a form of self-definition, and may symbolize lifestyle decisions about career choice or sexual orientation.

Body alteration and adornment are often used by women to mark a life transition and often conveys erotic appeal, marital status, genealogical background, and self-expression. Although only recently popular in America, body modification has long served these purposes in many other cultures. Moroccan women use henna to mark their hands and feet with elaborate designs as part of a marriage ritual. Although the markings fade within weeks they serve as both public announcement of the woman's change in social status and private codification of a life change. . . .

The physical change is also spiritual. [In her article "Moroccan Women's Body Signs," author Deborah Kapihaun notes that] the henna is said to contain *baraka*, a "divine blessing," that "works through the physical body to effect the metaphysical one." The henna marks are physical, spiritual, private, and social evidence of a new status. The hennaed woman also fasts, which enhances her ritualized process of physical, spiritual, and social transformation. In contrast to henna ceremonies that prepare a Moroccan woman for marriage, "secular" or non-marriage related henna ceremonies are self-initiated. These events emphasize self-expression and "signify sexual self-possession rather than initiation." The decorative designs establish the bearer's claim to her own body.

## Self-Stigmatization

Body alteration functions in similar ways in Western culture, but it accrues a different potency as a deliberate choice of identification because of the stigma it incurs as a rebellion against, rather than an embodiment of, dominant cultural values. American women, fully aware of the stigma attached to tattooing and body alteration that doesn't help achieve standard beauty goals for women, are more likely than men to choose adornment that is not publically visible and attach more personal meanings to their markings. In a culture that has taught them to preserve their bodies for the enjoyment of others, women who tattoo themselves are implicitly making a declaration of independence from at least some aesthetic standards expected of them by families, friends, and society. One 21-year-old woman explained the reaction of her mother to her tattoo. "She asks me to keep it covered if we go out in public. It is a sign of disrespect to her." [In his article "Memorial Decoration," author Clinton Sanders quotes] one woman [who] explained, "I did this not for my husband, not for my parents, not for a boss, not for anyone else but me . . . my internal reason was to make a statement." Women mark their bodies as an act of reclamation of their identity after a divorce, as a gesture of healing from sexual or other physical abuse, or simply as self-celebration. [According to Sanders] body alteration symbolizes "control over and pride in the physical self" for many women. Centuries ago, this tangible evidence of self-control and self-celebration may have been enough to convict a woman of witchcraft and sentence her to death. If a "devil's mark" was found on the body of a woman accused of witch-craft—whether self-imposed or organic in reality—it was interpreted as a chosen mark that confirmed the woman's autonomous nature and rebellion against prescribed behavior. Her willful desecration of her God-given body proved her collusion with the Devil. Today, a woman's self-creation carries less formidable consequences. Similar to the ways in which punk styles of "leather and metal access forbidden gender symbols and behavior," [according to writer Wendy Chapkis in her article "Beauty Secrets,"] for women, tattoos and piercings provide a form of gender rebellion. Taylor's 1970 study highlighted this idea when one of the woman subjects proclaimed her motivation to tattoo as "I want to act like a boy . . . anything they can do I can do better." Tattooing and body piercing blur previous assumptions about gender roles for both women and men.

## Cultural Defiance

Historically considered a salacious and pagan badge by Western cultures, deliberate body alteration proclaims defiance of cultural standards for both men and women, and many body modifiers enjoy the shock value of their adornment and take pride in their stigmatized identities. Piercees and tattooees reject mainstream norms of adornment while simultaneously embracing subterranean status. This is an especially important component of the body modification trend for adolescents who are trying to establish social identity and autonomy from parental authority. The decision to tattoo or pierce signals an attempt at rebirth in which the adolescents choose to become autonomous. Recreating the body differentiates one from one's previous childhood body, and conventional familial and cultural milieus.

One connection between body alteration and youth and popular culture is explained by Daryl "Bear" Belmares, who had been a professional piercer for nine years in 1996. Belmares attributes the rise in piercing popularity since 1990 to the influence of media and describes two general motivations to pierce. Some people are entranced by the trendiness of the look. "They come in and say 'I saw it on MTV.' They've seen the Aerosmith video that has a model with a pierced navel and think it looks sexy." Their main motivation is a desire to be different. These individuals are likely to let their piercing heal over after a few years. Other piercers are "functional piercers" who spend more time premeditating their decision and pierce for sexual enhancement, to consciously mark a transition in their life, or to heal emotional scars. Although one might think that women are more likely to pierce as a narcissistic use of the body to establish identity, based on the proportion of self-starvers and self-cutters who are women, Belmares denied this gender distinction, noting that his clientele is 50 percent men and 50 percent women.

## Piercing as Therapy

However, according to Belmares, women are more likely to pierce for therapeutic reasons. One scenario in which a woman pierces to heal an emotional wound might go as follows. A woman who has been sexually abused feels alienated from her body and sexuality. She does not feel in control of her past or her sexual expression; she feels like a victim. She is numb sexually, both physically and emotionally. This woman may choose a genital pierce to recreate and reclaim her body. If she is conscious of her motives then her choice to undergo a painful moment and a healing period is especially empowering. Even if she is not fully aware of her motives to pierce, she benefits from the process of integrating her psyche and body through an ornamental pierce. She may choose a piercing that enhances erotic sensations and cannot help but become aware of her body sensations as her body heals. During the healing period of several weeks she must wash her piercing twice a day, lavishing care on a part of her body and psyche that had previously been injured. As the woman's body heals, so does her sexual psyche. The woman has relinquished the role of victim to choose an identity that includes adornment and eroticization of her body. Her act of self-creation coincides with a realization that she can control many aspects of her sexuality, body, and identity. What was once numbed and detached, physically and psychologically, begins to feel alive again.

The body-art renaissance has sparked a sophisticated use of

body alteration as a source of identity and adornment [since the mid 1960s] although the general public continues to see these practices as deviant or at least unusual, especially if an individual shows interest beyond "acceptable" decoration, that is, a single tattoo or pierce. [In his book *Customizing the Body*, Clinton Sanders notes that] the association with deviance and unconventionality empowers body alteration to be "primarily a mechanism for demonstrating one's disaffection from the mainstream. Tattooing [and] body piercing . . . are employed to proclaim publicly one's special attachment to deviant groups certain activities, self-concepts, or primary associates." However, as body art becomes more popular, its relevance as a mark of unconventionality will change. One wonders whether the body art trend, which is already accruing many advocates and attention in the mainstream media, will be able to sustain its romance with marginalization, or whether it will soon become a mundane act of conformity. Already, pierced navels or single rose tattoos on a woman's ankle have lost the ability to shock.

## Seeking Public Identity

Although it is tempting to reduce tattoos to ornamental patterns imposed on the blank surface of the skin as expressions only of personal identity, past and current practices refute this simplistic interpretation. The message of a public tattoo is not only its content but its existence as a display of public identity. Symbols of identity that are used to construct identity in the eyes of others carry meanings far beyond their physical existence. "Self-symbolizing" as Peter Gollwitzer calls this self-construction and presentation, is based on the desire for an audience to witness the act or identity construction. Gollwitzer points out that individuals are more likely to self-symbolize during times of identity-related anxiety. This supports the interpretation of body alteration as confirming self-initiated identity and lends a clue to the proliferation of body art in our contemporary culture in which individuals constantly seek new avenues to declare their autonomy and uniqueness. Whereas once tattoos were considered marks of degradation, now individuals take pride in their self-stigmatization and publicly display colorful and elaborate tattoos. The difference between publicly visible and private identity marks is the degree of witnessing desired by the tattooee or piercee. This dynamic of self-construction that requires the observing power of a witness echoes the dynamics of narcissistic and sadomasochistic interactions that require recognition by another to confirm identity. Tattoos and other symbols of identity may reassure the bearer of an otherwise tenuous self-concept or reinforce an existing self-image. By completing a process of identity construction with a physical body change, one reduces the anxiety of liminality. Rather than having a community inflict marks of initiation, a self-marked person determines his or her own self-construction.

This self-construction is intimately tied to social perception. Regardless of the tattoo design, which may be a military insignia, a heart with a name, a tribal design, or any of an infinite number of unique and personally meaningful symbols, the tattoo is a declaration of uniqueness. Some people may have symbols, names or likenesses of heroes, relatives, lovers, or alter egos. Magical symbols, cartoon characters, family insignias, nicknames, faces of loved ones, or erotic pictures may be etched upon the skin. Others may have custom designed patterns or scenes. As permanent and public displays these body adornments simultaneously individualize the bearer and affiliate him or her with other body modifiers.

Although public perception is changing, a visible body mark is still symbolic of rejection of mainstream culture and its ethic of appropriate image and control of the body. In contrast to religious creeds that dictate reverence for God's finished work of the unmarred human body, body alteration glorifies the human body as unfinished, to be adorned and recreated. Only gradually is it becoming accepted as adornment and as a sign of self-proclaimed identity.

# 4

# The Controversial Nature of Body Art

# Tattoos Portray Life in Los Angeles Gangs

Elena Gaona

Tattoos have long been favored as symbols of identity in gangs. As mainstream culture has embraced the art form in the 1990s, tattoos have become even more prominent among gang members. According to the Los Angeles Police Department, tattoos are now common in gang youths as young as ten years old. Tattoos often reveal gang affiliations, prison backgrounds, and personal experiences that provide officers with important clues in gang-related investigations. In the following article for the *Los Angeles Times*, staff writer Elena Gaona explores the significance of tattoos in gang culture.

TO LAW ENFORCEMENT OFFICERS, GANG TATtoos are like modern-day hieroglyphics.

Gang detectives study the ink drawings, looking for everything from clues about crime suspects to signs that a youth may be unhappy at home.

"Tattoos are more popular in general, so now you see them even more with gang members," said Officer Richard Duran, a gang expert in the Los Angeles Police Department's Central Division. "Now you see really young kids are more tattooed, like 10-year-olds. That's the current trend." Some tattoos found on gang members are well-known. Authorities say the symbol of a black hand with a prominent letter M on the palm

■

indicates affiliation with the Mexican Mafia. Three dots in the form of a triangle placed somewhere on the hand mean "Mi Vida Loca" or "My Crazy Life."

Prison towers with clocks or numbers might reflect the years someone was incarcerated or "killing time," said gang Detective De Waine Fields of the LAPD's Hollenbeck Division.

Even seemingly artistic designs can give detectives clues. Women on the neck are "classic gang tattoos," said Detective Gabe Barboza.

Barboza said one neck tattoo popular with gang members is the image of a woman with flowing hair, striking eyes, large breasts and a slim waist. Designs also may cover markings left by drug use, he said.

Duran said gang members used to start getting tattoos in their late teens. In recent years, more have seemed to be getting their first ink markings as preteens, he said.

Tattoos could give parents insight about their children's activities, he said.

"I saw a 12-year-old who had [gang symbols] on the back of her neck, on her elbow and on her stomach," Duran said. "Her mother was oblivious to her being in a gang. I think she was in denial, like most parents."

Authorities said each tattoo can have several meanings. A teardrop near the eye can mean years of hard time in prison or represent fellow gang members who have been killed.

Of course, some tattoos have nothing to do with gangs, and simply being in a gang is not a crime, they said.

"A tattoo [can be] just pride in the neighborhood," Fields said. "I don't automatically think a guy is a gangbanger just because he has tattoos. You have to look at the totality of the circumstances."

## Street Canvases

Joey, a 25-year-old gang member from the San Fernando Valley who said he's been in and out of prison, said he was 13 when he got his first tattoo. He had long admired gang members with "eye-popping" tattoos on their chests.

The words "Trust No Man" were pricked into his skin to remind him of the first lesson he learned from his mentors. "I still don't trust nobody. Everyone I've trusted has stabbed me in the back," he said. "Not my homies though."

With each passing year, Joey gained tattoos that let him

# Interpreting Gang Tattoos

| Tattoo Image | Meaning |
| --- | --- |
| Clock faces without hands | Doing time |
| Tombstones with numbers on them | The years they were inside |
| Tombstones with numbers and RIP | Mourning the death of a friend |
| Spider or cobwebs on elbows or shoulders | Doing time |
| Eight balls | Behind the eight ball or bad luck |
| One laughing face, one crying face | Play now, pay later or my happy life, my sad life |
| SWP | Supreme white power |
| Peckerwood | White pride ( males ) |
| Featherwood | White pride ( females ) |
| Viking themes | Common Caucasian tat |
| Granite block walls | Time in Old Folsom Prison |
| 100% pure | Pure white or anglo |
| Cell window with sun or bird showing | Waiting to get out |
| Face of female crying | Has someone on the outside waiting |
| SUR | Southerner |
| Norteno | Northerner |
| Prison block wall with bricks falling outward | Inside wanting to get out |

"Tattoos: Recognition and Interpretation," by Ken Whitley, www.convictsandcops.com.

use his body as a canvas to tell his life. Joey says growing up with drug-addicted parents made him turn to friends on the street for support.

"I live life as a warrior because of what I believe in," he said. "I believe in where I'm from. At any moment I'm ready to die for it. That's why I'm all tattooed up, to let everyone know."

Generally, the presence of numerous tattoos representing gang life shows that "the gang is pretty much their whole life," said Thomas Ward, a lecturer of anthropology at the University of Southern California (USC).

That devotion is a reason tattoos become a form of expression and identity that is irresistible even if gang members know police keep track of them, Ward said.

"They're saying to the world, 'This is who I am.' To the cops they're saying they're down, deeply committed. They're in it for life, and 'There's nothing you can do about it.'" Ward said. "To the rest, they're saying 'I'm a gang member and I am to be feared. If you don't respect me, at least you will fear me.'"

## Messages Based on Personal Experience

Many tattoos are based on experiences. The right side of Joey's head has the most personal tattoo on his body. A pair of feminine eyes are crying, with the words "Only God Knows Why" written above the haunting gaze.

"My younger brother was shot in '98. He got shot in Boyle Heights," Joey said. "There were mothers and ladies crying. I know everyone had the same question: 'Why?' That's where I got the idea [for the tattoo]. Only God knows why."

The more distinguishable tattoos help police find suspects, said homicide Detective Rick Peterson. Witnesses are able to remember and identify people more easily when the tattoos are prominent, such as on the face or neck, he said.

Usually hard-core gang members get very visible tattoos, said Father Gregory J. Boyle, director of Homeboy Industries, a jobs program for former and current gang members in Boyle Heights.

Boyle said prominent tattoos on the face may mean the bearers don't care what other people think. They have no feelings about getting arrested for breaking the law, about being identified, about the future, about life, he said.

One gang member once walked into the office with an obscenity tattooed on his forehead.

"He'd effectively given up," Boyle said.

Ward said "[Gang members] with more tattoos can be saying, 'I need help. Rescue me from myself' is the subtext. They could be looking for support."

# Parental Involvement Is Tricky When Teens Want Body Art

Mary Lord and Rachel Lehmann-Haupt

With tattoos and body piercings increasingly sported by fashion models, pop singers, and movie stars, tattooing has become one of the fastest-growing retail businesses in the United States. As body modification has gone mainstream, practices such as branding and scarification that were once considered extreme have become commonplace in large cities across the United States. While teenagers are the primary patrons for these practices, the generation gap often leaves their parents feeling left out of the decision-making process and at odds with their own children. Mary Lord, a senior writer for *U.S. News & World Report*, and freelance writer Rachel Lehmann-Haupt explore the mine fields parents must walk when their teenagers want body art.

DOESN'T THAT HURT?" ASKS JESSICA BROWN, AGE 10½, as she rivets her gaze on the ivory spike through graduate student Shawn Arthur's nose. She stares at the needles skewering the skin on either side of his chest. "That's got to be painful."

Her parents, Mark and JoEllen Brown from Nanticoke, Pa., listen approvingly. After an afternoon of gaping at living canvases at the "Inkin' the Valley" body-art convention in Wilkes-

■

Barre, Pennsylvania, Jessica no longer craves a tattoo. She says they "make people uglier." She'll settle for just a navel ring.

## Body Modification Goes Mainstream

Jessica's parents might consider that a victory, given that teen-agers today seem to comb the National Geographic for fash-ion tips. (Don't laugh. Branding, scarification, and stretched earlobe holes are showing up among kids in California and New York.) Tattoos and piercing are far more mainstream than most parents realize. In a forthcoming study of more than 2,100 adolescents from schools in eight states, Texas Tech University School of Nursing Professor Myrna Armstrong found that 1 in 10 had a tattoo and that over half were inter-ested in getting one. The young "body-art" enthusiasts came from all income levels and ethnic groups. A majority earned A's and B's.

What's a parent to do? Many child-raising experts would have you believe that resistance is futile. It isn't. But the social and commercial currents are powerful. Tattoos and piercings have become widely acceptable, if not respectable. They turn up on celebrities, in toy stores (the Tattoodles doll), and as games on the Internet (Piercing Mildred [www.mildred.com]). Young Jessica can tick off every pierced part on her favorite pop singers, the Spice Girls. "I've got people bringing in pic-tures from Glamour magazine and wanting me to reproduce some star's tattoo," says Scranton, Pennsylvania, tattooer Marc Fairchild, who—like most professionals—refuses to work on minors. "Pamela Anderson [of TV's Baywatch] has made me thousands with that barbed wire around her arm." One Miss America contestant even bared a bellybutton ring in the 1997 pageant.

That's why tattooing emerged as the country's sixth-fastest-growing retail business in 1996—after Internet and paging services and bagel, computer, and cellular phone shops. [In the following nine months] the industry expanded by more than one studio a day, to 2,926—a 13.9 percent jump. These brightly lighted establishments are springing up near subur-ban malls and colleges. . . .

While it may alarm parents, the body-art fad is "nothing pathological," says University of Missouri psychiatrist Armando Favazza, an authority on self-mutilation and author of *Bodies Under Siege*. Indeed, studies show that young people indulge in body art for many of the same reasons adults do: to differentiate themselves, commemorate an event in their lives, or simply for the heck of it. "I like expressing myself that way—it expresses me," explains senior Tiffanie Gillis, a former varsity volleyball and soccer player at Piedmont Hills High School in San Jose, California. She sports a dozen perforations in her ears, a pierced bellybutton, tongue, and nipple, and five discreet tattoos, including a cartoon character she now regrets inking on her ankle two years ago, at age 15. Though her father has begged her to stop, Gillis intends to get more markings when she turns 18 and no longer needs to fake parental consent. "To tell you the truth, it's addictive," she says.

"Frankly, I like being shocking," says alternative music fan Amy Elizabeth Eisenberg, 20, a former scholarship student in marine biology at the University of Maryland who got the first of her eight facial piercings at age 16. "Why not?"

How about the pain? Though tattoo and piercing initiates often ask about it, most experience only a modicum of discomfort. Biting your tongue hurts more than getting it pierced. Tattooing feels like hair electrolysis.

## Emphasizing Health Concerns

Parents would do better to emphasize the potential medical complications. Navel piercings can take 12 months to heal, for instance, and can hurt for much of that time, since they are prone to infection and easily irritated by waistbands. Tongues, though quick to mend, swell tremendously when first pierced and can remain tender. "I had to live on Slurpees for a week," recalls Bridget McNicholas, a 14-year-old sophomore from Bowie High School in Maryland who had her tongue pierced. The health risks include hepatitis B and tetanus, as well as skin reactions that can occur with red and yellow dyes. An improperly placed piercing can damage nerves. Dentists have seen tongue studs cause problems from chipped teeth to speech impairment.

If a kid shows any concern about the pain, that could be an opening for parents to suggest faux piercings with magnetic studs or temporary tattoos such as mehndi (henna) skin paintings.

Though many states ban the tattooing or piercing of minors, parents can't count on that to protect their kids. Wily teens will find ways to thwart ID checks and permission forms. Tiffanie Gillis got a friend's father to accompany her to the tattoo parlor at 15; she then returned alone, using that first tattoo as "proof" she was of age. When Philip Wheeles, an 18-year-old senior from Gaithersburg, Maryland, and his girl-friend drove three hours to Ocean City, Maryland, for her to get her tongue pierced, . . . they grabbed a stranger off the boardwalk to sign the parental consent form. And those were legitimate establishments. Amateurs known as "scratchers," operating out of flea markets and fruit stands, rarely demand ID—or pay attention to hygiene. Kits that include needles and ink sell for a few hundred dollars through skin-art magazines.

Many teens resort to do-it-yourself jobs. Elizabeth Fisher, 15, an honors student in Manchester, Maryland, and her friend inked ladybugs on their ankles last summer. Her mother let her cover the mess with a professionally done blue bear rather than remove it. . . .

For the parent of the persistent teen, there is the risky strategy of a field trip. "Luckily, we ran into people who said what we wanted to hear," says JoEllen Brown, mother of pre-teen Jessica.

## Making Informed Decisions

Parents who feel they have exhausted all other avenues can still stress to their children the wise words of heavily tattooed rock star W. Axl Rose: Think before you ink.

"Start out small, and put it in an inconspicuous place," rec-ommends Steven Snyder, an Owings Mills, Maryland, derma-tologist and laser surgeon who has removed over 10,000 tat-toos. The bulk of his business is older people who have spent years regretting their youthful exuberance and keeping the ev-idence covered in long sleeves or folks who broke up with the partners whose names are emblazoned on their bodies. De-pending on the size and color—black ink is easier to remove than green—most tattoos take several painful laser sessions and cost between $800 and $1,600 to remove. Homemade jobs of-ten prove more difficult than a professional piece because the ink may get etched deeper into the epidermis, or leave scars.

If all else fails, parents can still try to protect their kids from major damage. Visit several tattoo and piercing parlors. First impressions count for a lot: If a place isn't clean, walk away. "Ask to see the autoclave," recommends Las Vegas tattooer Mari DeVine, who says no one has ever asked to see hers in the three years since she opened Tattoos-R-Us. These sterilizers work like pressure cookers and can kill hepatitis B. Needles should come in sealed packages and be opened in front of you. Each pot of ink or petroleum jelly should be fresh for you. Tattooers and piercers should wear latex gloves. Guns used for punching holes in earlobes are inappropriate for other body parts. "Most piercing shops are dangerous and have no concept of what they're doing. You have to be really careful," says Jhan Dean Egg, a San Francisco piercer.

## A Struggle Even for Experts

It may come as sweet consolation to learn that even the experts—tattooers, piercers, body-art enthusiasts—also grapple with dissuading their kids. "Ear piercing, that's where I draw the line," declares Jim McNulty, a heavily tattooed database administrator from Dickson City, Pennsylvania, whose 14-year-old, Ashley, wants to get a tongue stud and thinks navel rings are "the coolest-looking things in the world." For a tattoo, it's age 18 or no go. Reasons McNulty, "The larger tattoo is a decision on a lifestyle, not just what you want to wear on your body." Unless, of course, the whole point is to needle your parents.

# Working the Tattoo Underground

Camille Dodero

In the following exposé for the *Boston Phoenix*, staff writer Camille Dodero profiles Tex, one of Massachusetts's most popular clandestine tattoo artists. Although tattooing has been illegal in the state since 1962, talented artists like Tex operate thriving underground body art businesses that rely solely on word of mouth referrals. With tattoo prohibition laws rarely enforced in Massachusetts, the colorful tattooist often holds parties at which he tattoos many clients in succession. He has even given tattoos to some of the local law enforcement officers in the state.

A TATTOO WOUND OOZES LIKE CUT FRUIT, AND right now Andy Biagini's right shoulder has the complexion of sliced watermelon. It's a glossy mess of crimson ink, irritated skin, and microscopic punctures. Over the next few days Andy's upper arm will flake and peel, and in a few weeks his skin will have healed into the image of a bursting sun. At the moment, though, Andy's shoulder is still fresh and goopy.

## An Underground Tattoo Party

But he is not behaving like someone with an unbandaged abrasion. Sitting in his kitchen, the 30-year-old is twisting around on a stool, cracking open a can of Red Dog, talking to his friend Tom, and generally playing the role of a party host, which in fact he is. He and his wife, Sherry, are having a tattoo party, and there are 12 guests milling around their house, several of them eating chips, drinking beer, and waiting to do something completely illegal.

One of them, Andy's 23-year-old brother Steve, is having that illegal thing done right now at the dining-room table. One sleeve of his MARTHA'S VINEYARD CREW T-shirt is scrunched up to his shoulder, '50s greaser style. His exposed triceps is being cupped firmly by a hand in a latex glove; another gloved hand holds an electric tattoo machine above Steve's arm. The hands belong to a ponytailed man who calls himself Tex, who three hours earlier used the same machine to make hamburger meat out of Andy's shoulder.

Tex dips the ends of the machine's needles into a rubber thimble of black ink that rests on the table. Then he uses the machine to trace the outline of a flag on Steve's arm, the plunging needles injecting black pigment into Steve's epidermis. Tiny dots of blood bubble up through the skin's surface. Tex lifts the needles to wipe away the clotting blood with a cotton pad. When he looks up, Sherry is pointing to her husband's gooey shoulder and making a face.

"Andy, go wash it now," Tex says.

"Okay," Andy answers dutifully. He stands up, sees Steve's pale face, and can't resist teasing his brother a little.

"Why're you so quiet?"

Steve sighs. "I really don't feel like breaking out in song."

When I first heard about tattoo parties in Massachusetts, I didn't know what to expect.

## Marks of Rebellion

As trendy as tattoos are, they still carry the scent of the outlaw—the accumulated outsiderhood of generations of inked bikers, sailors, and convicts. And that scent is particularly strong here in Massachusetts, where tattooing has been against the law [since 1962]. The nearest legal tattoo parlors are over the border in New Hampshire and Rhode Island, and considering that many of these establishments are pretty sketchy—even though they're regulated by the Board of Health and employ licensed artists—I figured that underground tattooing would be, at the least, extremely seedy.

Except for one thing: the people who kept telling me about their tattoo parties weren't bikers. They weren't even edgy urbanites. They were friends of my family—suburban folks with mortgages hanging over their heads and swing sets in their . . . backyards. These people, as far as I knew, weren't into amphetamines or scarification. They had kids in dancing school and dogs named Pal. And they lived in residential neighborhoods like the one I'm driving through on my way to the Biaginis' tattoo party.

It's about 10 minutes past three on a Sunday afternoon in early September, and I'm following a 35-year-old father of three in his pick-up truck. He's leading me to the tattoo party—an event Sherry and Andy have agreed to let a reporter observe. The scenery makes me feel as though we're paying a visit to Old MacDonald: cows grazing by an eroded silo, two SLOW CHILDREN signs, a blinking yellow light, a farm stand, and, nailed to a roadside elm, a wooden sign bearing the hand-painted word ANTIQUES.

Accidentally driving past the party location, my guide turns around in the driveway of a church. We finally pull into a yard with a streetside red-flag mailbox. There are three cars and a mini-van already parked here. The air is fragrant with fresh-cut grass.

At the front door, I'm greeted by a pierced bellybutton. It belongs to Sherry, a petite blonde. Finding a piercing here in Pleasantville is like being in a foreign city and spotting a Red Sox cap—it's the familiar among the unfamiliar, a wink of recognition. And, to us, it's a sign that we're in the right place.

## An Outlaw Ink Slinger

I follow Sherry into the vestibule of the split-level house and up a set of stairs. She points diagonally behind a grandfather clock, over to the dining-room table, where Andy and Tex are seated. Andy has gelled black hair, is bare-chested, and looks like a *Grease*-era John Travolta. Tex has a silver handlebar mustache, more salt than pepper in his ponytail, and a weathered face that reminds me of actor Tom Skerritt. In his right hand, he holds what looks like an electric fountain pen but sounds like a drill; with his left hand, he cradles Andy's upper right arm. From my angle, it looks as if Tom Skerritt

126

is tightening Danny Zuko's shoulder.

Pointing to the man on the receiving end of the drill bit, Sherry does the introductions: "His name's Andy, and he's wincing in pain."

Then she motions to the ponytailed man with the tool and says, "You know Tex."

Tex is the reason I'm here. For the past 19 years, Tex has earned his living at parties like this one. His studio is wherever he happens to be. His office is his home. The mini-van out front belongs to him: it transports his sterilization pouches, his design sheets, and his tattoo machine from one house to the next.

Tex knows a handful of other underground tattoo artists in the state, but he can't think of anyone else who does it as a full-time job. For him, he says, the journey began with a bad tattoo that he got in his Nova Scotia hometown when he was a teenager. That's when he decided he wanted to try his hand at ink slinging. So he paid monthly visits to a shop in Toronto, hoping to learn the trade. And within a year, the shop's owner took the 18-year-old under his wing as an apprentice. Eleven years and thousands of customers later, Tex worked his first tattoo party in the Bay State.

"I met some guys off the Bar Harbor ferry," he says, "and we all got along well. They hung around for a few days and then they invited me down to Massachusetts to visit the Wareham area. So I made a trip down the following spring and then started coming down two or three times a year, doing these tattoo parties for just a handful of guys and their friends. They kept wanting me to come back."

## Meeting Heavy Demand

At that point, Tex did what any businessman would do: he recognized an obvious demand and met it. He moved to Massachusetts 17 years ago and soon established his own business as an underground tattoo artist. His business even has a name: Clean and Sober Tattooing.

Legally or illegally, Tex has been involved with body art for 31 of his 49 years. In the world of tattooing, he's considered an old-timer, a "grandaddy": he's been in the trade for all these years, he's spent time working in shops all along the East Coast. He's also a member of 12 tattoo associations. He's been a judge at "Marked for Life," the annual convention of female tattoo artists held every January in Orlando.

These days he does four or five parties a week. And he's booked solid [for the next four months], with a long waiting list of people hoping to get in sooner. . . .

"Ninety percent of my business," he says, "is repeat business. Word of mouth, that's all it is. When people see the work, they're like, 'Wow.' They're happy with it."

## A Loyal Clientele

And the people at the party seem to agree. In the middle of the afternoon, Tex beckons Sherry over to the dining-room table. "Sherry, I've been tattooing your family for what, about five years?"

Sherry: "Yep, it's been at least five years. And we've had you do body-piercing, too."

Tex: "And you've never had a problem with anybody or anything, have you?"

Sherry: "No, that's why I have you do it. Everybody's always been happy with their tattoos."

Tex: "It makes a big difference who does it."

Sherry: "I know. I've been very, very faithful to you, Tex." She turns to Cheryl, a mother of two, who got the cartoon character Ziggy tattooed on her ankle at the party. "Tex's done all four of my tattoos."

Cheryl: "He should have bumper stickers that say, 'Tex is the best!'"

Tex: "I do."

Actually, his bumper stickers proclaim that TEX IS THE TATTOO GOD, but the gist is the same. Tex has a loyal clientele and, like any businessman, he's not shy about self-promotion. He's got business cards. Bumper stickers. Refrigerator magnets. And if you reach his answering machine, the message is clear:

"Hi, this is Tex. Sorry I'm not here to take your calls right now, but I'm somewhere on the road pushing ink."

There aren't any statistics on the scope of the tattooing underground—"underground" isn't entirely a misnomer—but talk to people in the business and one thing quickly becomes apparent: Tex may be unusual in the wholesomeness of his operation, but he is by no means unique in what he does. Tex himself can rattle off a handful of people working on the South Shore alone. Shana Simpkins, a 23-year-old Brockton resident and tattooing apprentice at Inflicting Ink in Portsmouth, Rhode Island, can think of more. "There's two people who work in Brockton, and there's a girl in Stoughton," she says. "There's a guy in Boston whose work is pretty good."

Not everyone's work is all that good, however. With no state sanctions or Board of Health inspectors monitoring the field, tattooing in Massachusetts is extremely inconsistent—and potentially dangerous. For every Tex, there's a fistful of mediocre tattooists, people either who have little training or are entirely self-taught.

## Poorly Trained "Scratchers"

An untrained tattooist is known in the business as a "scratcher," the industry's equivalent of "hack." Despite the unseemly reputation of scratchers, people go to them for various reasons—primarily because they're cheap. Tex's rates, for instance, aren't too different from those at a legal parlor in Providence: at the party, he charges $90 for a three-inch shamrock on a forearm and $35 to retouch two faded flags on a biceps—in general, just a shade less than what you'd pay for similar work in Providence. A scratcher can and will dramatically undercut both prices. But, of course, there are risks involved.

"They order equipment out of the backs of tattoo magazines," says Shana Simpkins. "And they don't know what they're doing." She's not speaking just from the perspective of a paid artist, but also from that of a customer. "It's short money, real cheap, and they [the customers] will see [the tattooist's] work on somebody else and figure that the guy's all right. That's what happened to me.

"I went to this guy in Lawrence who works out of his house. And you know what his cards said?" She pauses, and then bursts out, "'Big Daddy's House of Pain'!

"But everything seemed right. I had seen his work on a friend from college and it was pretty good. He seemed cool, he had an autoclave and a copy machine. It was a good deal, real, real cheap.

"I had two silhouettes of a cat done on my shoulder blades

and it didn't hurt at all. I had them for a while and then I realized they were totally off-center. Then when I started learning more about tattooing, I realized that it [the procedure] didn't hurt because the guy used the wrong set of needles on me."

Simpkins says, "People just figure a tattoo is a tattoo, but it's not. And that's why people get fucked."

## Prohibition Laws Rarely Enforced

With that to contend with, it's no surprise that Tex deliberately distances himself from the wild side of tattooing. His approach is so open that some people seem unaware they're even breaking a law.

At the Biaginis' party, during a conversation about tattoo prohibition, a woman named Leigh interjects: "Wait, you're not supposed to get tattoos in Massachusetts?"

There's a prolonged silence, and no one seems sure how to respond. Finally Kurt, an employee for the town of Hanover who has stopped by to book his own party . . . coughs. "Well, there's no tattoo parlors."

"Does that mean it's illegal?"

Yes, Leigh, tattooing is illegal. But clearly there are degrees of illegality. A drug dealer who operated like Tex, with an answering-machine message that told callers, "I'm out on the road pushing crack," wouldn't be on the road for long. Tattooing is more on a par with, say, fireworks: you can drive over the border to get one, and there's little crackdown on illegal activity.

There's so little crackdown, in fact, that when I call a court employee to ask if anyone has been prosecuted for illegal tattooing in Tex's jurisdiction, she laughs. "I don't know how you'd find that out," she tells me. "Maybe it would be under 'prosecution of obscure laws.'"

Marie-Eileen O'Neal, a house policy coordinator in the Massachusetts Bureau of Health and Quality Management who has been dealing with tattooing for the past year, hesitates before responding to the same question. "You've got me," she says. "I've been asked a lot of questions about tattooing in the past year and that's the first time I've been asked that one. I've never heard of anyone being prosecuted. If there is an underground practice, it's itinerant, so law enforcement would only get involved if someone complained about it while it was in progress."

# Tacit Approval from Law Enforcement

But according to Tex, Massachusetts law enforcement *is* involved. Very closely involved: sometimes they're the ones getting inked.

"I've tattooed police chiefs in the state of Massachusetts," Tex says. "I've tattooed a couple of staties, but they've got too much cornstarch up their ass. I even did a couple of federal agents, and they're not supposed to have any [tattoos]."

"The cops know all about these guys," says Shana Simpkins, "but they don't care. They know it's a retarded law that shouldn't even be on the books anymore." She hesitates and then admits, "Even a cop I knew wanted me to tattoo him here in state, but I never drew him up anything."

As for Tex, he'll even go so far as to alert the cops he's coming to town. "Usually, before a party, I'll phone the police department or one of the guys on the force and say, 'Hey, I'm working such and such.' Yeah, why not?

"In Weymouth one time, I did a party for a whole family of brothers. One of the guys asked me, 'Do you mind working on police officers?' And I said, 'No, not at all.' He said that some of the guys who worked at the police department, which was across the street, wanted to get work done. So I said, 'Holler out the window and tell them to come over.'

"So they called over. One guy came over to watch me work. He was in uniform and on duty. His wife wanted one. He was asking the normal questions, 'Is everything clean?', all the worry questions. Then he called his wife over, and she got a peach from an Allman Brothers album cover. She was real happy with it. He wasn't. He really didn't want her to get a tattoo. He had called her over figuring that once she saw the operation, she wouldn't get one done.

"I do several parties for these same people. Next thing you know, I've got a sergeant there, getting one that he got in the Navy redone. And I've got a lieutenant standing there, next in line.

"Then this guy who was upset with his wife [for getting the peach tattoo] comes to the door. He's joking around with the guys, but he's not crazy that his wife's got the tattoo. He looks at me and says, 'Well, what would you do if I was to bust your ass?'

"And I said, 'You're going to have to wait for me to finish the sarge first. Then, my gear is safe here, I've got a houseful of cops, so I'm going to walk across the street, I'm going to pay my fine, and I'm going to come back here, and I'm going to say, 'Next.'"

## Tupperware and Tattoos

During the Biaginis' eight-hour open house, friends and family members flow in and out in a constant tide. Two Tupperware bowls of Doritos and a box of Roche Brothers chocolate-chip cookies sit alongside a veggie platter on the kitchen counter. There's Coke, Diet Coke, Red Dog, and Sprite stocked in the fridge.

Some guests, like the Ziggy woman, show up with their own tattoo designs in mind. Others find their tattoos by flipping through Tex's dog-eared portfolios, a series of leather-bound booklets with hundreds of laminated design sheets displaying a vast repertoire of possible images: suns, dragons, butterflies, coyotes, tribal art, buxom nude women, zodiac signs, animals with horns, fangs, and pitchforks. There's a demonic Sonic the Hedgehog, a blood-soaked Michelin Man, and—my personal favorite—a Big Bad Wolf sodomizing Little Red Riding Hood.

And all the while there's somebody glued to the kitchen chair, biting his or her bottom lip, silently praying to God (or, in Andy's case, "the gods"), and pretending not to be fazed by the permanent staining of his or her skin. Gradually, partygoers become desensitized to the tattooing procedure, and by nine or ten at night, the person in pain is peripheral to the party itself.

Over the course of the party, 25 people stop in, 11 people are tattooed, and more than $650 in cash changes hands. The police don't show up. The most excitement comes at 9 p.m., when a woman drops her can of Red Dog on the floor. ("She's a three-beer drunk; she'd be a cheap date," Tex later jokes.)

There has always been a social element to getting a tattoo, so on some level it makes sense for illegal tattooing to take place in this setting: in a house, at the dining-room table, among friends and family. And for the most part, a home is more comfortable and less intimidating than a cold, stale legal parlor.

Given the intimacy and aesthetics involved in getting a tattoo, choosing a tattoo artist is analogous to choosing a beauty salon: people take their business to the places their friends and families recommend. And that's why Tex doesn't worry about competition or legalization. As long as he's left alone, illegality doesn't constrain his lifestyle or his grassroots enterprise. And the arrival of legalized shops wouldn't remove the engine that drives his business—his word-of-mouth relationships with people. Considering the permanence of a tattoo, that's more important than a license.

"I do what I want to do," he says, "and that's that."

Rufus C. Camphausen, *Return of the Tribal: A Celebration of Body Adornment, Piercing, Tattooing, Scarification, Body Painting.* Rochester, VT: Park Street Press, 1997.
This book explores the tribal elements inherent in all forms of body modification—from piercing and tattooing to scarification and genital mutilation.

Jane Caplan, ed., *Written on the Body.* NJ: Princeton University Press, 2000.
This volume offers a variety of viewpoints on the changing significance of tattoos across history and cultures. Essays explore tattoos from their mythological roots in ancient Celtic society to their popularity as marks of self-expression in the contemporary United States.

Margo DeMello, *Bodies of Inscription: A Cultural History of the Modern Tattoo Community.* Durham, NC: Duke University Press, 2000.
DeMello traces the evolution of tattooing from its primitive Polynesian roots, through its rise in popularity within the working class, and finally to its current vogue status in popular culture.

Jim Gerard, *Celebrity Skin: Tattoos, Brands, and Body Adornments of the Stars.* New York: Avalon Books, 2001.
Gerard offers the inside stories on celebrities and their body modifications. The book includes over one hundred color photographs of the beauty marks of the stars.

Steve Gilbert, *The Tattoo History Source Book.* New York: Juno Books, 2001.
Gilbert has compiled an exhaustive collection of historical records of tattooing throughout the world from Greek and Roman times to the present. The book chronicles tattooing as witnessed by explorers, journalists, physicians, writers, anthropologists, and even tattoo artists themselves.

Bonnie B. Graves, *Tattooing and Body Piercing (Perspectives on Physical Health).* Mankato, MN: Capstone Press, 2000.
Citing the latest research on tattooing and body piercing, Graves offers strategies for informed decision making. The book includes

a brief history of body modification, a description of the procedures involved, and an overview of associated health risks.

Kim Hewitt, *Mutilating the Body: Identity in Blood and Ink*. OH: Bowling Green State University Press, 1997.
Hewitt argues that many individuals in modern culture are using their bodies as canvases—marking and altering their bodies to express autonomy and spirituality.

Amy Krakow, *The Total Tattoo Book*. New York: Warner Books, 1994.
Krakow provides a comprehensive overview of the modern practice of tattooing, including the evolution of tattooing as a business, the social issues surrounding the practice from the 1880s forward, and the intricate workings of a tattoo studio.

Victoria Lautman, *The New Tattoo*. New York: Abbeville Press, 1996.
This comprehensive book on the art of tattooing traces the origins of the earliest tattoos, explains the evolution of the tattooing profession, examines themes for current tattoos, and answers questions about getting or removing tattoos.

Madame Chinchilla, *Stewed, Screwed and Tattooed*. Fort Bragg, CA: Isadore Press, 1997.
Tattoo artist Madame Chinchilla chronicles the history and lore of tattoos, including the social stigmas and spiritual meanings associated with the art.

Nan McNab, *Body Bizarre, Body Beautiful*. New York: Simon and Schuster, 2001.
The author traces body decoration from its ancient roots to its modern manifestations, identifying how and why people have altered their bodies across the ages.

Maureen Mercury, *Pagan Fleshworks: The Alchemy of Body Modification*. Rochester, VT: Park Street Press, 2000.
Mercury argues that body modification practices are primitive reactions against modern technological society and that both the rituals and the symbols of body art offer practitioners the opportunity to reconnect with their bodies and access the divine.

Margot Mifflin, *Bodies of Subversion: A Secret History of Women and Tattoo*. New York: Juno Books, 1997.

Mifflin provides a comprehensive account of the complex role women played in tattooing in twentieth-century Western culture. The author identifies colorful women characters from tattoo history and argues that tattoos have offered women a powerful form of self-expression.

Jean-Chris Miller, *The Body Art Book: A Complete Illustrated Guide to Tattoos, Piercings, and Other Body Modifications.* New York: Berkley Publishing Group, 1997.
Miller explores all facets of tattooing and piercing, from why people modify their bodies to how body modifications are done.

Laura Reybold, *Everything You Need to Know About the Dangers of Tattooing and Body Piercing.* New York: Rosen Publishing Group, 1996.
Stressing the permanence of body modifications, Reybold identifies the various health risks and social consequences faced by tattoo and body piercing practitioners. The author advises anyone considering a body modification to exercise extreme caution when making the decision.

Arnold Rubin, ed., *Marks of Civilization: Artistic Transformation of the Human Body.* Los Angeles: Museum of Natural History, 1988.
This scholarly text provides a historical overview of body modification practices in many cultures around the world.

Ronald D. Steinbach, *The Fashionable Ear: A History of Ear-Piercing Trends for Men and Women.* New York: Vantage Press, 1995.
This text offers a broad historical and cultural overview of ear piercing. The author covers such subjects as the acceptance of earrings in work and school environments and the religious and legal implications of ear piercing.

Samuel L. Steward and Phil Andros, *Bad Boys and Tough Tattoos: A Social History of the Tattoo with Gangs, Sailors and Street-Corner Punks, 1950–1965.* Binghamton, NY: Harington Park Press, 2001.
Coauthor Phil Andros, who gave up his career as an English professor to become a tattoo artist, chronicles the American tattoo scene of the 1950s and early 1960s, a period in which the tattoo subculture was both marginal and tough.

Maarten Hesselt Van Dinter, *Tribal Tattoo Designs*. Boston: Shambhala Publications, 2000.

Offering anthropological background to the currently fashionable tribal motifs in tattoo design, Van Dinter explains how primitive societies' myths and customs influenced modern tattoo symbols.

Beth Wilkinson, *Coping with the Dangers of Tattooing, Body Piercing, and Branding*. New York: Rosen Publishing Group, 1998.

Wilkinson explains the health, safety, and legal factors one should consider before getting a tattoo or body piercing. The text includes a brief history of body art, motivational factors for body modification, and individual stories and experiences.

Daniel Wojcik, *Punk and Neo-Tribal Body Art*. Jackson: University Press of Mississippi, 1995.

Wojcik explores the symbolism and subversive aesthetic of punk body piercing, tattooing, and scarification. The author traces the development of punk body art from the inception of the punk movement in the early 1970s through its grunge and gothic manifestations in the early 1990s.

# INDEX